Risk and Adventure in Early Years Outdoor Play

Education at SAGE

SAGE is a leading international publisher of journals, books, and electronic media for academic, educational, and professional markets.

Our education publishing includes:

- accessible and comprehensive texts for aspiring education professionals and practitioners looking to further their careers through continuing professional development

- inspirational advice and guidance for the classroom

- authoritative state of the art reference from the leading authors in the field

Find out more at: **www.sagepub.co.uk/education**

Risk and Adventure in Early Years Outdoor Play: Learning from Forest Schools

Sara Knight

⑤SAGE

Los Angeles | London | New Delhi
Singapore | Washington DC

SAGE Publications Ltd
1 Oliver's Yard
55 City Road
London EC1Y 1SP

SAGE Publications Inc.
2455 Teller Road
Thousand Oaks, California 91320

SAGE Publications India Pvt Ltd
B 1/I 1 Mohan Cooperative Industrial Area
Mathura Road
New Delhi 110 044

SAGE Publications Asia-Pacific Pte Ltd
33 Pekin Street #02-01
Far East Square
Singapore 048763

Library of Congress Control Number: 2010938479

British Library Cataloguing in Publication data

A catalogue record for this book is available from the British Library

ISBN 978-1-84920-629-7
ISBN 978-1-84920-630-3 (pbk)

Typeset by C&M Digitals (P) Ltd., Chennai, India
Printed in Great Britain by the MPG Books Group
Printed on paper from sustainable resources

MIX
Paper from
responsible sources
FSC FSC® C018575
www.fsc.org

Contents

Acknowledgements

My grateful thanks are due to the different organisations who have allowed me to use my photographs of their settings: Bishops Wood Environmental Centre, Bridgewater College, Chelsea Outdoor Nursery School, Eastwood Nursery, Mid Suffolk District Council, and Roehampton University. Thank you to the staff, pupils and parents at Nayland School who continue to welcome me whenever I drop in to join in their outdoor sessions. I would also like to thank my friends and colleagues at the Green Light Trust, and at Anglia Ruskin University, whose support have helped develop this second book. And, as always, thanks to my husband David for his long-suffering patience and critical eye.

About the Author

Sara Knight is a senior lecturer in the Faculty of Education at Anglia Ruskin University, a Forest School level 3 practitioner, and a founder committee member of the Institute for Outdoor Learning Forest School Special Interest Group. Trained as a drama teacher but with gardening grandparents, Sara has found working with children in the early years an excellent way to combine creativity with a love of the outdoors. Sara ran her own nursery class, then worked in a Special School before moving into the FE and HE sectors. Alongside this, she worked with the Green Light Trust in Suffolk, latterly launching Forest School across the eastern region, running her own Forest School sessions and being involved with training. In 2009, she published *Forest Schools and Outdoor Play in the Early Years* (London, SAGE).

List of Figures

Introduction: Why Adventure, Why Risk?

Chapter objectives

In this introduction, I aim to:

- explain the objectives of the whole book
- describe why opportunities for risk and adventure are essential for normal development in the early years
- outline how this can be achieved
- describe how each chapter adds ideas to this agenda for every early years setting.

My previous book, *Forest Schools and Outdoor Play in the Early Years* (Knight, 2009), described ways in which children from the age of two can move out of their manicured play spaces and into wilder areas. In that book, I also described a child-led approach where play should, as far as possible, be 'freely chosen, personally directed and intrinsically motivated' (Conway, 2008), something requiring a more flexible perspective on planning. The Forest School approach encompasses this play-based introduction to wilder and riskier play, and I hope I explained why I thought that this was essential for the healthy development of children.

I still believe this to be the case, but I have become aware whilst training early years practitioners that not all of them are ready to embrace this message. There are some who are very nervous of the contemporary push towards more outdoor play, and the encouragement from advisors and others to provide more opportunities for children to take risks and have adventures. This may be because they are anticipating opposition from managers and colleagues, or because they feel that they lack the necessary expertise. In this book, I hope to help the nervous to move closer to wilder, riskier play, by describing the steps by which children of all ages can take the risks appropriate to their ages and stages. Some may feel that they lack the skills necessary to support children in riskier and wilder play. Whilst I cannot provide training in additional skills in a book, I can point out what can be done with only basic knowledge of the outdoor environment, and identify possible sources of training for interested practitioners.

My focus in the chapters will be grounded in practice, with what I hope are realistic suggestions. I have seen, done or bullied students into seeing or doing all of them. Chapters 1 – 7 explore ideas loosely based on natural themes, interweaving theory and practice, including some practical activity ideas. I will take one activity idea from each of these chapters into Appendix 2, where I will explore curriculum links, to offer ideas about documentation.

Chapter 8 continues the discussion of what risk means to different children and settings that I start in this section, so that practitioners will be able to see how outdoor experiences in the early years can develop into future opportunities for outdoor activities. I will offer suggestions about how to manage risk, with the caveat that the best way to start is by looking to see what is already in place in your setting.

The reference list is an important resource to settings planning to take risk and adventure on board. It contains references to theory, to help construct arguments to convince funders, parents and others that what you are planning is a good move, but also a percentage of books and articles that offer practical suggestions to settings ready to change. Similarly, the appendices are designed to help. Appendix 1 is a repository of some of the places to look and people to contact for resources in the UK. And, as stated above, Appendix 2 links some of my activity ideas to the Early Years Foundation Stage (EYFS), the curriculum for the under fives in England (DfES, 2007).

As you can see, the whole book is aiming to wrap the reader in a cosy blanket of 'can do', to enable all children to have the chance to engage with the environment in a deep way.

Risky play

Why are opportunities for risk and adventure essential for normal development in the early years? I will explain below why I believe this to be important, but I can start by assuring you that it is not just me saying this. Let me offer you a random set of statements from the EYFS (DfES, 2007):

- 'Through play children can ... take risks and make mistakes' (Guidance, p. 8)
- They can 'make choices that involve challenge, when adults ensure their safety' (Guidance, p. 27)
- Practitioners must offer 'opportunities to use a range of tools safely' (Statutory Framework, p. 14) and ensure 'safety without stopping reasonable risk taking' (practice card 1.4)
- Enabling environments offer ... 'a range of activities which will encourage children's interest and curiosity, both indoors and outdoors' (Guidance, p. 75)

- They can 'build and balance' (Guidance, p. 79)
- Practitioners will 'build children's confidence to take manageable risks in play' and 'plan activities that offer physical challenges' (Guidance, p. 90–1)
- Children will 'show understanding of the need for safety when tackling new challenges' and 'avoid dangerous places and equipment' (Guidance, p. 95)
- They 'learn to assess risks with help from adults' (practice card 1.3).

When you consider that the EYFS was written before the latest flurry of publications about the importance of risky play, it is encouraging that the DfES went as far as they did. Here is a clear exhortation to practitioners to grasp the nettle of the tensions between their fears and concerns and their knowledge that without exposure to risk, children will not learn to keep themselves safe. Who knows how brave they would be if it were rewritten today, three years on?

Neither I nor the EYFS are exhorting unsafe practice. As well as the statements listed above, the EYFS is also full of directions to undertake risk assessments (Statutory Framework, p. 33 and practical guidance, p. 17 are two examples). Through my own Continuing Professional Development (including my Forest School training) I, too, have learned to risk assess all aspects of my own practice, and would always suggest that practitioners do likewise. In Chapter 8 on risk and danger, I will explain ways to do this. Without opportunities to challenge themselves, children's understanding of safety will not move forward. So instead of saying 'No' to risk, try saying 'Ok, how can I do this happily?'

It is important that you help the children in your care to develop their understanding of safety, which is a many-layered thing. In part, it is about self-awareness. 'Where do I start and finish?', 'what can my body do?', 'how well can I control my actions?' are questions that we see the tiniest babies wrestling with as they grasp at toys and develop their mobility. This is an ongoing process, and young children are pre-programmed to keep stretching themselves, in the same way that all young animals do, until they reach maturity and the peak of their own particular set of abilities. The role of the adult, animal or human, is to enable the stretching process to be manageable and safe enough – in other words, to help them to take reasonable risks. The risks will vary according to the child's understanding and ability. For a new walker, an uneven surface will be a reasonable risk. For a new climber, a log on the ground will be sufficient to balance on. Competent walkers will appreciate dramatic differences in levels, competent climbers more adventurous trees or frames. Once the child's competence exceeds our own, we may need to call on an expert to move them on further still. Not to give them the early experiences may be to deny them the opportunity to reach their potential. It is shocking to think that many new walkers will only experience concrete or carpet beneath their feet, and will not learn to deal with uneven ground or sand until they are older. This will mean that when they go to the beach or run through snow or leaves, the sense of their own capacity, or lack of it, may pre-programme them towards undue risk taking or undue caution. Either way, it may affect the rate at which they gain physical competence or intellectual understanding of risk and consequence.

Why is this learning so important? Tim Gill (2007: 15) identifies four arguments in support of risk in childhood:

1   helping children to learn how to manage risk (understanding safety)
2   feeding children's innate need for risk with reasonable risks in order to prevent them finding greater unmanaged risks for themselves
3   health and developmental benefits
4   the building of character and personality traits such as resilience and self-reliance.

Another outcome from such opportunities could well be to engage children at a sensory and intellectual level with their environment, benefits observed by the Forestry Commission's research (O'Brien and Murray, 2007). In a world where climate change will be a real issue within their lifetime, it is important for children to connect with their environment at every level, and as often as possible.

How can all children access such opportunities?

For animals, it is a simple progression from incompetence to expertise in physical activities, as they do not appear to have such a complex psychology to wrestle with at the same time. The self-awareness of our species adds to this development the need to develop self-confidence and self-esteem at the same time, without which physical development can be inhibited. This is where early years practitioners are uniquely placed to mediate the pressures from family, culture and community and to give every child the opportunity to stretch themselves and maximise their potential. This is not to put yourself in conflict with parents, but to help them to realise, for example, that having the opportunity to go out in the rain helps children to understand more completely the world around them. Having your own understanding that getting wet will not of itself give you a cold will help. If you do not feel confident in this, find a speaker for a parent event who is. Local authority advisors, Wildlife Trust representatives and British Conservation Trust co-ordinators, are all people I have used to convince reluctant parents that I have the best interests of their children at heart.

Another aspect of understanding safety is knowledge. Knowledge is power, in this case the child's power to keep themselves safe. Even very young children can enter into a discussion about a feature of their environment that could offer them a challenge. When I take three-year-olds into the woods for Forest School sessions, we spend a lot of time talking, before, during and after the sessions. For some of them, a wood is in itself scary, being dark and unknown, and I want them to benefit emotionally, intellectually and physically. A child can't do that if s/he is scared or if s/he is unaware of danger. Bravery is not about rushing in blindly – it is about knowing the risks and doing the best you can. So we talk about nettles and brambles and holes in the ground, amongst other things that are a part of that environment that they will need to learn to manage. We do not remove them.

In settings with outdoor spaces, the challenge for practitioners may be to review the space and to think about ways to increase the risks, rather than minimise them. A concrete square has few visible risks, and yet children fall or push each other over and accidents happen. It may even be that some of the 'accidents' are the result of the limitations of the space, a direct correlation with the sterile safety being offered to the children. Perhaps if they had the challenge of a pile of logs to scramble over, the risks would be focused, could be discussed and managed, and learning could take place. There is a thought that if children have exciting, reasonable risks to undertake, they will be less likely to find unreasonable ones for themselves. This may be one reason for encouraging older children to undertake Duke of Edinburgh awards (DofEA), etc. Consider a pile of logs as an appropriate mountain for younger children to climb, and free-flow play between the indoor and outdoor areas as appropriate changes in temperature and climate for this age group to learn to manage. Children who learn these lessons early may move on to successes with DofEA or similar. Children who do not may get their thrills from balancing on the parapets of bridges.

Other settings may be fortunate enough to have a patch of grass. A flat piece of grass has few visible risks, but children run into each other, trip over balls and accidents happen. Perhaps if a great big scoop were dug out of the middle of the grass patch to make a hollow to roll into, or fill with water and make mud pies in, the risks would be focused, could be discussed and managed, and learning could take place. Just think of the proto-science, mathematics and physics that could take place in such a space. Risky activities can mean moving water around, perhaps in sections of guttering. It is not tidy, clean or micromanaged, but it is fertile ground for tomorrow's creative entrepreneurs. Getting dirty is a wonderful learning experience that we should all be allowed to have.

Some settings have no outdoor space at all, and have to rely on outings, but these, too, can offer opportunities for risk. They are just

Figure 1   The author's niece completes the 2009 London Marathon

different risks. If children have to make their own sandwich as soon as they can manoeuvre the tools, they are learning to take care of themselves. The risk is in the choice of fillings, and the likelihood that it will fall apart. If they have the responsibility for carrying a rucksack in which their spare jumper or water bottle can be carried, they are becoming more independent. The risk is in losing or forgetting the rucksack. This is apart from all the other risks involved in going out (which are too numerous to explore here).

Recently, my niece (in her twenties) asked me why I thought she enjoyed outdoor activities so much. I said I thought it was to do with the fact that as soon as she could walk, her mother took her and her brother to 'parent and toddlers' in the next village on foot, over a mile away, sharing the single pushchair. Her habits of exercise, established early, have continued and now include completing the London Marathon (see Figure 1). Not many children today have that kind of fitness as a start in their lives, for a number of reasons. For many of them, it is now down to their early settings to provide them with outdoor activities. It is our outdoor activities – in other words, our outings, the climbing and the digging that the children engage in – that will provide our children with the good habits of healthy exercise. We owe our children the right to develop their defences against obesity, heart disease and diabetes. I hope to demonstrate that even our youngest children can start building these skills and aptitudes, and that we owe it to them to provide these opportunities.

 Points for practice

Start planning for more adventurous play by undertaking an audit of what you do outside already. Write down all the outdoor opportunities that occur in a week for all the ages in your settings. Then look at their developmental stages. Which activities allow them to consolidate their fine and gross motor skills, and which allow for experimentation? Which (to use a Vygotskian term) are in their zone of proximal development (Holzman and Newman, 2008), and need an adult to scaffold success?

Now do the same for the other areas of development. Then consider how you can enrich what you do already to make it more exciting, and more open to children's experimentation.

 Discussion points

Discuss these points with your colleagues now, and then return to them after you have finished the book:

- Do you know the risk assessment policy in your settings, and how they are reviewed?
- What risky and adventurous activities do you offer to your children?
- What are the attitudes of colleagues and parents to risky play – can you find out?

Further reading 📖

Ball, D., Gill, T. and Spiegal, B. (2008) *Managing Risk in Play Provision: Implementation Guide*. Nottingham: DCSF.

Ryder Richardson, G. (2006) *Creating a Space to Grow: Developing Your Outdoor Learning Environment*. London: David Fulton.

Tovey, H. (2007) *Playing Outdoors: Spaces and Places, Risk and Challenge*. Maidenhead: Open University Press.

1

Earth

Chapter objectives

In this chapter, I aim to:

- consider the properties of earth as a medium for play
- explore the potential of mud
- discuss the topography of settings
- look at the opportunities for risk and adventure.

Introduction

Tactile play is a staple of early years settings. We know that this is one of the earliest ways in which very young children learn about their world, and is the way we make contact and express affection with each other throughout our lives. It provides comfort, knowledge, stimulation and pleasure. Tactile activities are used to support development with children who are difficult to reach, and with adults who are traumatised. We hold hands in times of heightened emotion, and hug each other at important moments. We cannot truly understand the nature of an object or a setting unless we can make contact with it – which is why all the informative television in the world cannot replace an actual experience. So it is that as we live on the earth, we need tactile contact with it.

In settings we provide tactile play. Sand and water play are commonplace, and we each provide our own favourite variants, such as cornflour and water, 'slime', finger paints, etc. With younger children, we also acknowledge the sensory value of babies playing with their food, and we know that feeling it squidge through their fingers encourages their manipulative skills (DfES, 2007: 57). We take messy activities outside in the summer, in order that they do not create as much mess indoors, and to offer opportunities for extensions such as foot painting. We are missing the main tactile ingredient that the outdoor environment offers us.

Earth is all around us, but usually we don't pay it very much attention. It is described as dirt, grit, mud and other such derogatory terms. It is something to wash off our hands, scrape off our boots and wipe off our coats. And yet it comes in an amazing variety of colours and textures, and is our constant partner in outdoor play. It is not only brown. Sit and look at some earth, and see how many colours you can see in it. Earth is one of the things that most children love and some adults don't, a theme that will recur throughout this book. This may well have something to do with the 'earth + water = mud' equation, so we will start by confronting this prejudice head on, and consider the potential of mud. Some will feel that there is a risk element here, which we will consider.

After mud comes digging. As a child, I spent holidays on the wide beaches of north Norfolk, constructing canal systems and castles – something I will return to in the next chapter. Here I will write about digging the earth to create changes in levels, with bridges and roadways, digging that increases team-working skills and cooperation. This will develop into links with Chapters 2 and 5. This digging can be an adventure, to create something new and big and together.

I will then consider the value of changes in levels in general, such as those created or discovered by adults to make the topography of the area to be used more interesting, followed up in the Points for practice section. This will lead into consideration of the opportunities for engagement with earth in the wilder environment, and the adventure element that is inherent in it.

Mud and its potential

The EYFS (DfES, 2007: 57) talks about using gloop, etc. to encourage mark making with very young children. Figure 1.1 is a demonstration of spontaneous mark making by a three-year-old. Not surprisingly, it is the first letter of her name, her personal identifying mark. When children have learned the first letter of their name, they like to practise it and use it, often to express their presence and sense of belonging or of ownership. She has used sticks, as the earth that day was hard (which gives a better contrast for the photograph), but on other days the stick became the tool to make marks in the mud. Consider mud as both a slate and a clay tablet. Here are links to the history of writing, as well as to the development of writing in young children. The expression 'ontology echoes phylogeny' roughly translates as 'the development of the individual echoes the development of the species'. So it is that the

Figure 1.1 My name is Anya

youngest child makes marks into a soft surface (food, mud, clay) and with sticks, as our ancestors did before the invention of paper. As they grow older, the mark making becomes more ornate, and it carries a clearer meaning.

It is difficult for us to know what the meanings of marks made by babies and toddlers are, if there are any, but we know that the rehearsal of the marks is an important part of the development of writing, just as the marks in clay tablets found in archaeological digs had meaning in ancient civilisations, and in some cases were the precursors of the forms of writing we use today. This is a roundabout way of saying that our youngest/least able children deserve opportunities for exploring mud, too! By doing so, they are developing concepts of what mud is and what it can do as well as strengthening muscles and developing the flexibility and control that they will need for manipulating and writing. Heuristic play will be covered in Chapter 6, which will include further consideration of the practicalities of enabling this to happen.

Mud comes in so many forms. At a simple level, it is a smooth surface that enables the youngest children to experience the qualities of a mud floor. It is often cool, it is rarely as hard as concrete and it makes a good surface for dancing on. You can use it as a clean slate to provide a background for creations and collections. On a hot day, it will cool you if you lay on it.

Mix in more water and it becomes more malleable, but its properties will depend on what the soil is that you start with. Light soils do not stick together like heavy clay soils, which is an interesting discussion point with older children. It also links to Chapter 5, where gardening is talked about. Heavier soils can be moulded more easily, and malleable mud can be an artistic medium. One popular activity is called muddy faces, described in the activity below. It can also be a building medium, creating small walls, or a substitute for refined clay, making bricks, pots or candle-holders. This last category is one where practitioners can sensitively extend ideas in order to develop children's skills, once they have exhausted the sensory experience of squishing the mud between their fingers.

As with all new experiences, children should not be rushed into making something before they have finished exploring the qualities of the medium. As Jensen and Bullard (2002) report:

> our favorite memories revolved around a common element – unstructured time spent playing outdoors. Many of us recalled sensory, messy, creative activities.

The feel of the raw materials, and the way they change as they are put to use is the first lesson about the nature of the materials, and one that needs full concentration to extract the most from the experience. It needs uninterrupted time, and opportunities to experiment, so that the full muddiness of mud is understood. This is so important that it may need to be repeated – do you still stand in mud puddles and rock your feet to make the mud move, to gauge its texture and consistency? If not, try it, and do not deprive your children of repeating this experience each time that they go out.

This reminds me of an outdoor session one muddy Ash Wednesday (the day after Pancake Day or Shrove Tuesday). Nearly all the children had had pancakes the night before, and there was much discussion about fillings and flavours as we walked to the wood. Many of the children seized on the opportunity afforded by the mud, created by several days of rain, to scrape up handfuls and mould them into pancakes. The adults were kept busy deciding on their favourite fillings and 'eating' the pancakes offered. This was a rich opportunity, both for language development and for emotional bonding, the shared play recalling the community experience in spontaneous child-initiated play. For some, it was the start of complex role play, for others a diversion soon tired of on the way to other play opportunities.

We can link this event to the exploration of mud as a therapeutic element. So far we have largely considered using mud in our hands, but as adults we might have had mud facials and mud baths. Perhaps this is going too far in settings! But children can have the opportunity to enjoy walking through mud in the summer, with it squeezing between their toes, or to jump in it in the winter, and see the splashes.

Activity: muddy faces

There are variations on this activity, so it should be adapted to suit the ages and stages of the children, and developed along their lines of interest. In its simplest form, mud or earth is collected in a bucket – if stones can be avoided, this is a good thing. Water is added to create a stiff paste – too much, and the faces will slide; too little, and they won't stick.

Take a handful of the paste, knead it in your hand, and then slap it onto a tree. You can use a fence post, but the rougher surfaces give a better adhesion. Find sticks, leaves, etc., to turn the blobs into faces.

You can use these to start stories, or however you wish. See Figure 1.2 for an example.

When we discuss the safety of using mud, hazards can be identified and dealt with in the same way as with any activity, and we will look at this in more detail in Chapter 9. So it is that we know babies will put the mud in their mouths, because that is how they learn about it. Individual practitioners will need to consider the quality of that mud – if it is likely to contain faeces, for example, it may not be the best mud for babies – and the age/stage of their babies, as well as considerations of whether it is the best time of year to undress them enough to enjoy the experience.

There will be a need for explanations to parents and discussions with colleagues the first time this happens. These are not reasons to 'protect'

Figure 1.2 Muddy faces on a tree

children from experiencing mud, but each practitioner will need to feel comfortable that they can manage the situation to ensure that it is in the best interests of the children in their care. There *will* be a summer's day and a bowl of freshly mixed mud that will provide the right chance. And on a cooler day with naturally occurring mud, older children will enjoy jumping in it, stirring things into it and scooping it into pots and pans to 'cook'. Washing hands afterwards should suffice for them to make the hazard a reasonable risk.

Digging

Many children like to dig. In the first Forest School that I ran, a group of four-year-olds began an earthwork project. I think it started with one boy digging a hole; it certainly had nothing to do with any of the adults. Soon there were six children (not all boys) working under the leadership of the first boy to create channels with bridges and tunnels that ran over a wide area of cleared forest floor. Where an obstacle occurred, such as a tree root, they discussed how to overcome it as a committee, and then one or two worked on that section. There was no water to move, no cars to drive down the created grooves, just the intrinsic pleasure of creating this interlinking network, which went on over three weeks. At the end, the game faded away, and the next heavy rain started the process of smoothing it into memory. While it had been going on, observing adults (none of us were invited to join in) could see team work, cooperation, problem solving, negotiation, planning, reflection and many other valuable skills being practised and developed. One child did wear a hole in his trousers, and quite a bit of ivy was cleared, but they were the only casualties. The developmental value of the project was immense. All we had provided was a space, one that could be utilised as the children wished and then left alone until the next visit, and some strong trowels and hand forks, plus time and freedom from interference. And as well as all the skills that were exercised, there was knowledge, about the nature of construction and about the environment: the earth, the tree roots, the ivy, and in the end, about the effects of the rain.

Forest School provides opportunities for all ages to spend time on their creations, something that otherwise is restricted to children in the Foundation Stage. Time is a precious gift that early years practitioners can offer their children, so it is worth considering whether you, too, have a space in your outdoor setting that can be set aside for a project to evolve over time. The group working skills that such a project offers are of huge value, particularly at a time when many practitioners are reporting behavioural issues that often stem from children's inability to communicate and work together. The fact that it may look less than lovely or even somewhat untidy to adult eyes is far less important than the life skills that are being learned. Perhaps a 'men at work' triangle would help deter adults from tidying up ongoing construction schemes. These projects can constitute an adventure, as children take ownership of creating something together, and take emotional risks in negotiating, planning and dealing with failures as well as successes.

Digging for a purpose may follow on from just digging for creative pleasure, or may be more attractive to some children rather than making empty canals. Gardening is one such activity, one increasingly finding a place in our schools and nurseries. In Steiner schools in particular, children may have opportunities even in their earliest years to grow food and then eat it. I will return to this theme in Chapter 5. Another purpose for digging is to move water around, which can stimulate a range of developmental opportunities. Making watercourses will be covered in Chapter 2.

In this section, I have described activities suitable for three-to five-year-olds (and above), but there are many opportunities for younger or less able children to help them connect to the earth. You will need to find implements for smaller hands to dig with. Plastic is not the best option; whilst plastic shovels, etc. will cope with sand, when used in earth they can snap, leaving sharp edges and frustrated children. In Appendix 1, I have included some suppliers who stock proper tools scaled down for smaller people. The less dextrous and skilled the child, the more important it is to provide them with the correct tools made from good-quality materials and designed for their size of hands.

Earthy slopes, often in wilder areas

Natural spaces where the earth is less likely to be flat provide more opportunities for adventure and risk associated with the earth. Sliding down a muddy slope is one such opportunity, described in the activity below.

 ### Activity: slippery slopes

First locate your slope. It should be long enough and steep enough for you to feel comfortable that your children will enjoy sliding down it without exceeding their capabilities. It needs to be bare of vegetation other than grass. One that ends in a small ditch is good, and if you have a water source to hand you will be saved the labour of carrying containers too far. You will also need some strong plastic sacks for the children to use as mud sledges. Water the slope to give a surface for sliding. The aim is for the children to slide down the slope seated on a plastic bag. You may need to tow/push the children until they develop their own techniques, and you will need to keep the slope watered. They will be learning about balance and steering, braking and rolling, as well as about the slipperiness of muddy slopes.

Figure 1.3 The dragon at Bishops Wood

Slopes are also useful to roll or run down, but getting to the stage where that is a reasonable risk can take time. Simply negotiating slopes can be a risky adventure for new walkers. Settings can help by providing early opportunities with small hills and tunnels. Figure 1.3 shows a construction where a 'dragon' has been laid down on a flat play area, creating slopes and an underground space for a secret den (dens will be referred to again in Chapter 8). Smaller, simpler mounds will also provide opportunities for learning to balance on slopes, and the kinetic play possibilities of slopes, rolling wheeled toys, etc. In this way, when children encounter natural slopes that may be steeper, they will have the genesis of the skills for dealing with them, and will not find them so intimidating. In time, they will have developed the confidence to tackle other sloping scenarios, and know how to keep themselves safe.

At this point, I would like to refer readers back to the introduction, to reinforce this message. Children need diverse experiences to draw on, to create an internal map or schema of how to deal with similar experiences in the future. These give them confidence, not only for the specific instance, in this case of dealing with slopes, but in more generalised terms. They will have learned that difference is not necessarily frightening; it should be examined and given a chance to be interesting and exciting, too.

〰️ Points for practice

In the introduction, I suggested that if you want to make your outdoor play more adventurous you need to start with an audit of activities offered. Practitioners considering the potential use of earth in their settings need to progress to an audit of their space. Whether it is a flat piece of tarmac or a square of grass, it is possible to make it more interesting, changing levels in different ways and adding in some earth. The aim would be to keep the materials used as natural as possible, as these offer more variety and flexibility as well as helping children to connect with the world around them.

When redesigning an outdoor play space, or starting anew, good practice means that practitioners should consult and find out what clients, in this case children, want. This can be difficult with very young children, who will naturally be constrained by their experiences of spaces so far. You can record their needs by observing their play in a variety of circumstances and analysing what their behaviour and responses are telling you about the constraints on their opportunities. You can use pictures and visits with the children (and with fellow practitioners) to develop these leads into suggestions. The Forestry Commission's Roger Worthington has a booklet *Nature Play: Simple and Fun Ideas for All* (2008) which gives some easy ideas. Lancaster (2010) suggests other ways to consult with children, and gauge their opinions. Do not limit initial explorations with practicalities. Only when you know where you and your children want to be should you start to consider how to get there, and it may have to be in stages, but it is better to succeed slowly than to compromise quickly.

The DCSF Play Strategy (2008) means that every council in England has a Play Builder scheme, developing play spaces in your area. Some of these are very imaginative, and it is worth contacting your play builder and finding out about new play provision in your area, to see if there are opportunities for your children to access more adventurous opportunities than will fit into your space.

Once you have access for your children, you will need to consider whether to provide protective clothing for them. There is no such thing as bad weather, only bad clothing (Knight, 2009: 16), and similarly getting dirty is a natural consequence of being outside, so it should be managed, not avoided. Appendix 1 gives some suppliers who provide suitable clothing for young children.

Discussion points

Discuss with colleagues what you can achieve to enable earthy play in your setting:

- Can you add a mound or dig out a dip?
- Could the mound be hollow, if you started with a concrete pipe, for example?
- Could the children dig into the sides of the dip to create interesting gullies and holes?
- Can you make a space for mud?

Further reading

Casey, T. (2007) *Environments for Outdoor Play: A Practical Guide to Making Space for Children*. London: Paul Chapman.

Elliott, S. and Davis J. (2004) 'Mud pies and daisy chains: connecting young children and nature', *Every Child*, 10 (4). Available at: www.earlychildhoodaustralia.org.au (accessed 13 March 2010).

Jensen, B.J. and Bullard, J.A. (2002) *Community Playthings: The Mud Center – Recapturing Childhood*. Available at: www.communityplaythings.com (accessed 17 March 2010).

2

Water

Chapter objectives

In this chapter, I aim to:

- consider the diversity of our children's encounters with water
- discuss extending watery play in settings
- look at ways of encountering water in the natural environment
- explore the potential hazards and risks of water.

Introduction

Water is a unique substance in that it constitutes at least 80 per cent of our being, which could help to explain its fascination. We have 'tame' water to drink and to wash in, but as an untamed element we frequently fail to control it. It is therefore important that children develop their respect for water with an understanding of the risks as well as enjoying the adventures it offers. I will start my exploration of this medium with the water most accessible to settings, namely with rain, and with commonly found receptacles such as buckets and watering cans. Staying in settings, I will then look at shallow water and how we can use it.

Consideration of shallow water includes managing access to ice and frost, which occur in settings where shallow water collects. These have caused debates in the UK recently, around permitting the creation of ice slides in playgrounds. Shallow water also includes creating bubbles, smell pots and the creation of mixtures from collected objects plus water.

My next section is about running water, which leads to gutters, gullies and streams. I will suggest ways to enable children to use the first of these adventurously in your settings, and we will think about streams in our 'wilder' section. This watery play can link the wilder areas of the outdoor environment to the more domesticated areas. I will also consider the risks of deep water, and how important it is to help children to keep themselves safe through their awareness of puddles that can get deep, and of how deep water collects behind obstructions. We will also think about floods and ponds.

Floods, dams, puddles and ponds flow on to beaches. I am concerned that worries about health and safety are restricting children's access to beaches, and will debate this fully, describing what I believe to be an important opportunity.

Rain, sprinkling and spraying

As a small child, I was convinced that if I sprinkled water onto the garden path (usually as the result of jumping in a puddle) rain would follow, in order to continue making the sprinkling pattern. The fact that it did says more about the local climate than about my magical abilities. Rain is fascinating for children; if you do not believe me, watch them watching it and then reflect on what they are seeing – the spontaneous and unplanned falling of drops of water from the sky! This has to be a rather magical phenomenon when you see it as a new experience. It saddens me that so many children are now conditioned by the adults around them to be almost afraid of going out in the rain. The myth that you can catch a cold from getting cold and wet has surely disappeared amongst qualified staff, but some folk memory seems to linger on.

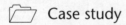 Case study

A four-year-old (dressed in waterproofs with only her face exposed) at one Forest School informed me that she was getting wet. It was raining quite hard, so I agreed. Realising that I was sanctioning this, she ran off and rolled in long wet grass, coating herself in wet grass seeds and bits of greenery, laughing excitedly. She realised that it was OK to get rain-wet, and was taking full advantage of the situation to really experience what that meant. Hopefully, this became a part of her cognitive understanding of a rainy environment, but definitely this was an emotional and sensory event, a connecting experience with her immediate elemental environment.

When we returned to nursery, she needed a complete change of clothes, which her mother had sent as the class were familiar with Forest School and its outcomes. Thus, practical planning enabled this child to push her boundaries, to take a risk and move beyond the norms of behaviour for her family.

Some people are currently missing out on the kind of experience described in the case study. Students who are timetabled to come outside with me moan if it is raining. My response is usually either 'Drips don't get wet, they get bigger' or 'You won't swell up and pop'. I can be deeply sympathetic! We are privileged in most of our settings by having access to warm buildings, changes of clothes and waterproof outer layers, so there is no excuse for not experiencing and, eventually, hopefully, enjoying rain. If we do not have these things, we need to plan how we will get them. As practitioners, we have a duty to enable young children to go out in the rain and then for them to work out what to do about it. Of course, I do not mean that we should do so in an uncaring or thoughtless way that will leave them cold or wet for a prolonged period, but I do suspect that much of today's practice is more connected to adult responses to rain than to a consideration of opportunities for children.

I wonder if the fun to be had from sprinkling and spraying comes from a need to 'scientifically' explore around the ideas generated by rain. Piaget saw children as mini scientists, perhaps as a result of observing this type of play. Do different-sized holes in containers create different-sized droplets of water, or just a different flow? This play may evolve spontaneously from watering plants, or see the activity below for a starting point. Carrying out such opportunities outside enables the play to be bigger and messier and more experimental, building on the activities provided in more conventional water play units indoors, where of necessity the play is smaller and more contained. Some children, often boys or children with motor control issues, benefit hugely from the opportunity to be unconstrained by rules designed to keep floors dry and thus safer indoors. They can be single-minded in their creativity and inventiveness, which are skills that the next generation will need as adults if they are to be successful in the twenty-first century (Duffy, 2006: 6).

 ## Activity: sprinkling and spraying

Collect a range of different-sized plastic containers and make different-sized holes in the bottoms. Try to ensure a good range, some big with big holes, some big with small holes, etc. so that the size of the container is not a predictor of the size or number of holes. Start the experimental play with a suggestion that the children transfer water from a container in one part of your outdoor space to another in another place. The addition of sections of hose and funnels will increase the opportunities.

This activity involves no risk, but is a huge intellectual adventure around conservation of mass, of flow and other scientific and mathematical concepts. This can help stimulate the engineering brains of the future!

Shallow water

The consideration of rain naturally leads on to the consideration of puddles, which are likely to be the first naturally occurring shallow water that children will encounter. I advocate jumping in puddles, naturally, although it is helpful to have on the right footwear, and to be aware of the dangers of deep puddles, something we will consider later in the chapter. Puddles in settings can be used as something like a paint pot, using sticks, brushes, small spades, etc. to tease the water out into patterns and pictures. These will then disappear at different rates, according to the ratios of water, wind and sun, prompting opportunities for discussions and stories.

Similar 'magic painting' can be done on vertical surfaces (walls, fences) using pots of plain water and brushes. The head teacher of a large nursery occupied the minds and bodies of some lively four-year-old boys by telling them that a witch was about to attack the school, and the only defence was to paint around the outside of the building with this magic paint. By the end of the day, they were tired but victorious. There was fuel for several days of storytelling, too, stimulating the language skills of the children. These adventures of the imagination stimulate developing creativity in constructive ways.

Frozen puddles create patches of ice, potential risks for the unwary. This is when it is so important to take the opportunity for learning, rather than remove the entire hazard unexplored. Small children who learn that puddles can be slippery are learning lessons that will keep them safe in the future. The youngest will need to be held and supported in their explorations, and as they grow in experience they will develop their awareness of the nature of ice and how to manage it. If this experience is available to them, then by the time they reach school age, they will be able to start to judge whether they have the skills to slide on it. They may fall over, too, which is a part of the learning experience, giving both scientific and physical lessons.

Of course, there is a balance to be struck, so managing the risk is essential. One icy puddle saved for experimentation and clearly marked out will not put visitors to your setting at risk, for example, as adults are more at risk from falls than children are (HSE, 2010). This can be seen clearly in countries where children learn to manage ice and snow at young ages, and the damage from falls is less dramatic for children than when adults attempt to learn the same skills at an older age. Discussions about ice on ponds will continue later in the chapter.

Other forms of shallow water can include water features – see Figure 2.2 below. These features offer some of the excitement of water without the risks, and so are popular for areas that are not always closely supervised. They can therefore make a valuable contribution to the wet resources in

Figure 2.1 Very young skiers in Sweden

a setting, provided that they *are* a resource, and not just a decoration that cannot be used by the children. Because of this, it is important to select a design that can be easily cleared of materials added as experiments by the children. The beauty of such designs is that because they are 'closed systems', it is often possible to add colour or bubbles to the water to stimulate new ideas. Bubble making can be a highly creative activity but as the only risk is in ingesting small amounts of the solution, I will only mention it here as a part of wet play in settings.

Slightly more risky is the concoction of smell pots, a very popular activity (see the activity below).

 Activity: smell pots

Equip your children with something like an empty yoghurt pot, and send them to collect samples from their favourite bush/tree/plant/flower with cautions about protecting the plant by only picking small amounts. Encourage them to add small amounts of water to

(Continued)

(Continued)

their pots and mash up the contents to release the natural oils into the water. Compare the scents.

Extension activities include the blending of natural perfumes and the mixing of potions for imaginative play. A discussion about not tasting these is advised.

As with all outdoor activities, there are benefits in encouraging children to consider the risks by undertaking them with the help of practitioners, rather than leaving them to 'discover' the risks by trying them out on their own. I can recall mixing rose petals into an unappealing brown soup in my own childhood attempts at natural perfume – fortunately not something I ever felt inclined to ingest! We will revisit the risks from plants in Chapter 9.

Figure 2.2   A water feature at Eastwood Nursery

Running water

We have already talked about moving water in leaky containers. It is so much more successful to move water in specially designed channels. Many settings are now providing sections of guttering to help with the movement of water around the outdoor spaces. A few have hollowed branches to make the process even more exciting, and aesthetically more pleasing to adult eyes. Figure 2.3 shows one such at Bishops Wood Centre.

Activities to explore the flow and direction of water can be very stimulating for children, the major risk being upsetting tidy-minded caretakers and managers. It is then the responsibility of practitioners to justify an outdoor play space that has some features in common with a builder's yard. One practitioner related that it took her a term to persuade her caretaker to leave the construction materials where the children had left them in order to allow work to recommence the following day. The activity below gives some ideas for play of this nature. Richard Louv (2010: 81) describes the learning that comes from construction play, which validates it as a rich learning opportunity. I would also like to validate it as a way to make contact with a natural force that we can wonder at, in all the ways that it moves and all the things it can do. Variations on the above will accommodate adventures with flowing water in most settings. Those with enough space will also be able to cope with the creation of gullies that will take water, either similar to those described in Chapter 1, or made in sand. Once out in wilder spaces, the opportunities become different, and the running water is most often that in a stream or ditch.

Figure 2.3   Natural water channels

Activity: using guttering to create a flow

Equip your setting with some lengths of guttering. Plastic guttering is easy to find in DIY stores in the UK in a variety of lengths, but branches hollowed to provide a water channel are more interesting. You will also need other construction materials to hand, such as building blocks, for the channels to balance on. As in the sprinkling and spraying activity, the ultimate goal may be to move water from one point to another, or it may be to transport boats and other floating craft along the channels. You will need to enable a fall from the starting end (a) to the finishing end (b), so your water source (a) needs to be higher than the collecting vessel (b). Set the children the challenge to arrange the channels in such a way to enable the flow of water or vessels. Discussions will occur about ways to manage the joins to minimise leaks. You can overlap piping, or if they have ends you can have a waterfall from one to the next. Or you may try using sealing materials such as plastic bags or clay. The size of the potential adventure is only limited by the imagination of the participants.

With younger or less experienced children, you may choose to start on a smaller scale, by setting up a closed length on the ground for them to experience. Once the potential for play is subsiding, raise the structure slightly so that you can elevate one end and allow flow from the other end into a bowl, providing a jug to carry the water back from the bowl to the elevated end.

If you are going to spend any time in a wilder space, you will have visited it beforehand and done a risk assessment. One of the things you will have looked at is the likely source of any water your children will have access to. Fortunately in the UK, the pollution levels in naturally occurring water flows are considerably lower than they were, and generally if they are clear they are clean enough to play with, provided hands are washed before eating. Beavers have nothing on children who are interested in shifting the course of a stream, or damming it to create a deeper pool to wade in.

This leads to an important learning point about the risk of deeper water, whether it is in puddles or streams. Children who play in streams learn about how to judge when water is deep. As a country child, I learned that my eyes could deceive me when it came to the depth of clear flowing water. I used to test the depth of the water I waded through with a stick, checking in front of me continually until I knew the section I played in. I do not know how I learned that trick, or who from, but it stopped me walking where the water would go over my wellies many

Figure 2.4 Ford and bridge

times. This is a skill you can teach your children when they are old enough to wade in streams, or along water-filled ruts and tracks. Perhaps then when they are older, they will not drive their cars into floods as so many have done in the recent UK floods. A potential site of risk can be seen as Figure 2.4. This bridge and ford design is not that uncommon, and in summer it is safe to walk or drive through. The photograph was taken in March after rain, and although the silt has had time to settle so that the water is clear, the depth is deceptive, in places dropping to deeper than half a metre. Many car exhausts would be submerged, and many wellies filled. In addition, the flow is enough to push over an unwary child.

The bridge in Figure 2.4 is ideal for playing pooh sticks, a game described by A.A. Milne in his Winnie the Pooh stories. All players drop a stick of their choice into the stream on the upstream side, and turn to the downstream side to see which comes out first. The physics of the relationship between the size of the stick and the flow of the stream, and the effects of being in the middle or at the side, or caught in an eddy have, I am sure, been the subject of a dissertation somewhere in the Western world. For younger children, the wonders of the game are sufficient.

I am hoping that you will feel encouraged to seek out running water for your children. In your walks, you may encounter streams and water-filled ditches that will offer opportunities for play, and you can either help to replicate some of these in your settings, or will find a place where your children can experiment in wilder areas. Falls of water are found less often in the UK, but they are magical places, and some even have hidden spaces behind them. They are more risky to access, having faster flows and wetter, slipperier rocks, so you will need 1:1 ratios for children in the Foundation Stage if you are going up close. But these enchanted places will leave a long-lasting memory, helping even in a single visit to connect children to the natural world.

Deep water

Pools and ponds in settings are often covered in netting, which can destroy their beauty and eliminate their play value. It is understandable – we know that we can drown in the amount of water that it takes to cover the mouth and nose simultaneously – in other words, not much water – so deep water needs to be watched. But this means that to have a close encounter with deeper water, children must usually go out of their settings. One exception that I have found is at the Chelsea Open Air Nursery School, where the pond is covered by a grid strong enough to take the weight of the children and big enough for them to be able to reach into the water and to do pond-dipping activities (see Figure 2.5).

Figure 2.5 The pond at the Chelsea Open Air Nursery School

Fortunately, lakes and ponds in parks are not netted, so we can visit and learn the basics of safety as we bombard the water birds with food offerings. And in country areas we can walk around natural ponds and lakes, and the man-made reservoirs of differing sizes. As we explore them, children are learning from us about soft edges that might not support our weight efficiently, about the uncertainty of the depth of water (and the soft mud under still water). In winter, they learn that the ice that looks so solid probably isn't, and that the competency to judge its strength is learned over time and not even all adults can do it. In other words, they are learning about the nature of risk and how to manage it, in a natural and organic way. Sobel (in Louv, 2010: 185) describes this process of learning from nature as linking back in our minds to our simpler selves from millennia ago, when we learned all our knowledge this way, and which makes the process more deep-seated and memorable. They are important lessons for today, particularly as climate change means that more of us are likely to need to be able to manage deep water in the form of floods.

Lastly in this section, few of us working in the Foundation Stage will have the opportunity to take our children onto boats on running or still water, but the water safety that we help them to assimilate will stand them in good stead when such opportunities do arise. These are enhanced by their play *with* boats (small ones), be that in settings or on the water spaces we access.

Beaches

All of the activities talked about so far can happen on the beach, plus so much more. Beaches are special, possibly because they are 'between' places, between the land and the sea, neither one thing nor the other. Just as the half light of dawn and dusk create between times, so a beach creates a between place. Betweenness creates uncertainty – is it light, or is it dark? Is it wet or is it dry? Uncertainty heightens our awareness – the primal flight-or-fight awareness of adrenaline. In that state we see and feel deeply. So we collect shells and stones that seem beautiful, but when we get them home are less shiny and special. Dropping them in water reminds us of the wonder they held, and allows us access to memories. Visits to beaches, for many of us, are still something to savour beforehand and hold in memory afterwards.

We associate beaches with holidays, times when grown-ups might be more focused on play and relaxation. This means that special rules can apply, about clothing and about what is allowed behaviour. Children rely on the adults around them to scaffold that behaviour, which gives practitioners the opportunity to convey important safety lessons around things like the use of inflatable toys on beaches – in the UK, these seem to be at the root of many accidents that occur – and the understanding of tides and currents. Digging holes and making sandcastles are normal things to do on UK beaches, and where there are rock pools there are even more opportunities, to watch and observe miniature worlds as well as to search for crabs and anemones.

In France and the southern European countries, it is still possible to see early years groups on the beach, equipped with sun umbrellas and windbreaks as necessary. In the UK, this seems less so. Talking to practitioners, it would appear that a fear of risk is stopping some day nurseries from taking children to the seaside. As those children may be in the settings from eight in the morning until six in the evening for up to four years, this reluctance may deprive those children of their chance to connect to the beaches closest to where they live. Their beach knowledge will come from holidays that may be in other countries, and therefore their understanding will be that the best beaches are in foreign lands, not part of their country's environment and therefore of less concern to them. To bring them into more familiar range, we need to visit our nearest beaches, and find out what they hold for us.

Walking on sand, paddling in the sea and peering in rock pools are simple steps to take, but important ones. For example, there is so much to find out just about sand – how to walk on it, wet and dry, how to sit on it or stop it from getting everywhere or use it as a construction material. This largely sensory learning is transferable to other places and times. It will be necessary to prepare properly, for example there is a helpful leaflet 'Group Safety at Water Margins' available on Teachernet (www.teachernet.gov.uk) which suggests precautionary measures, but this additional effort should not preclude making the valuable experiences of beaches available to children.

Points for practice

You have been asked to audit your activities for risk and adventure, and to audit your space for opportunities for those activities. In this chapter, we have been looking at additional resources brought in to the setting, and I suggest this is a good time to look at the resources you have to facilitate adventurous play in your settings.

Adventurous play tends to be robust, and therefore it needs robust equipment. In Appendix 1, there are lists of some of the suppliers of child-sized real tools. Plastic replications of adult tools are not strong enough and will frustrate rather than support the children. In my nursery, I had a woodworking bench with proper sharp tools on the basis that sharp tools cause fewer accidents than blunt ones. We had rules to follow and adults to instruct, to ensure the correct usage, and in this way the children made objects they could identify and use in their play. In Forest School, children learn at a young age to use the best tools for the tasks they wish to undertake.

Similarly, if children are constructing water-carrying channels in the outdoor setting, the materials need to be appropriate to the task. Shopping for them can be a part of the adventure. If you can find natural materials that will do the job, then the effects will look more pleasant to the eye, and are likely to be more sustainable, as well as introducing children to ways of using the resources nature provides. The wooden water channels cut from branches are a good example. To find these in the UK, you could try contacting your local environmental education department or nearest Forestry Commission office.

Discussion points

Discuss your watery play with colleagues to make it more adventurous:

- Do your water play toys include a range of sprinkling and spraying containers?
- Can you enable the children to play with flowing water?
- How often do you visit other watery places (streams, lakes, beaches)?
- Is there any continuity between your watery play and your other activities, such as your reading materials?

Further reading

Little, H. and Wyver, S. (2008) 'Outdoor play: does avoiding the risks reduce the benefits?', *Australian Journal of Early Childhood*, 33 (2): 33–40.

Louv, R. (2010) *Last Child in the Woods*, 2nd edn. London: Atlantic Books.

Warden, C. (2004) *The Potential of a Puddle*. Auchterader: Mindstretchers.

Air

Chapter objectives

In this chapter, I aim to:

- consider the elusive quality of our children's encounters with air
- discuss ways to make air a tangible presence in settings
- look at ways of encountering air in the natural environment
- explore the risks and adventures in encountering air.

Introduction

If we are all in contact with the earth around us, as stated in Chapter 1, then how much more so are we in touch with the air we breathe every moment of our lives? And yet we cannot see it except by inference from the movement of other things, and only touch it if it is disturbed, and smell it if there is an addition to it. But it is an essential part of our natural world, and therefore something to be aware of, to respect and to protect. In this chapter, we will think about ways to make this element manifest to our children, in order to heighten their awareness of air as a part of the world about us.

A good starting point to help children of all ages to see the effects of the movements of the air is to encourage them to lie on their back and look at the sky. The moving clouds create images that can be spun into stories, and if they are under trees the tracery of the branches can make other shapes to create other stories. It is worth taking time to do this, firstly to watch and wonder at what you and the children are seeing, and then to discuss and record the stories and pictures you or they create. Perhaps you can see where Jack climbed the Beanstalk and reached Cloudland?

The wind can affect the behaviour of humans and other animals, making them restless or skittish. Then there are Buddhist prayer wheels which respond to the movement of the air and have a special significance, or sounds from wind-driven Aeolian instruments that have an eerie quality that stimulates the imagination. So in this chapter about air, I will pick up on ideas about our awe and wonder of an element that we cannot see, but one that affects our moods and behaviour and can be very powerful. After all, it was the wind that took Dorothy to Oz.

There are many stories linked to things of the air, such as clouds, kites and the wind. The adventures of stories are deep in all cultures. The risks are about allowing ourselves to be carried along with them. These are rarely physical risks (unless children try to copy a dangerous storyline), but there can be emotional risks in stories, particularly for children under the age of six, when they are still wrestling with the boundaries between fact and fiction. Practitioners need to be sensitive to these risks, and help the children find their own way through them without crushing their excitement. After all, we all need to hold onto Father Christmas or his equivalent for a while. Similarly, respect for cultural and religious beliefs are important when spinning stories, and every setting will have different sensitivities to accommodate.

Storytelling places

It seems that the air holds many stories, which is perhaps why the word 'inspire' means to breathe in (air) as well as to create. As I am dealing with storytelling in this chapter, this is a good place to discuss an outdoor storytelling space. Storytelling is another way of connecting children with their surroundings, and is regaining its popularity, as can be seen by the number of storytellers at events and festivals. The act of storytelling is about the spinning of tales relevant to the children and to the place they are in, and each one will be subtly different, even if the starting point is the same. Stories can also be used as therapy, through sharing, allegory and metaphor, and storytelling is the oldest way to pass on our cultural heritage.

 Activity: storytelling

Seek out and create an area where you feel comfortable telling stories to your children outside. It might be a shady corner where you can throw down a blanket and some cushions, or it might be an exciting old chair you can set up in a willow arbour. Whatever space feels right for you and your children is a good one. Start with a story you know well, and if it helps to have some objects to act as

(Continued)

(Continued)

props, take them out with you. Do not start with too many children in your group, particularly if they are very young. If they are babies, it may well be best to be one-to-one. When you are comfortable with telling the story, you can invite older children to invent changes to the storyline, adding or subtracting plot, characters, scenes, etc. It will be your shared adventure. Once you have done this a few times, and feel more confident, you may like to consider creating a more permanent storytelling area. You will know by then what works for you, and how to create your special place. Do not be surprised if you find the children in there without you, telling stories together.

Practitioners may not feel comfortable about telling stories without a book to rely on at first, and storytelling does not replace the comfort of reading and re-reading familiar books, but it is worth having a go, and telling stories when you are outside is an easier place to start than indoors. For a start, you have the richness of nature to inspire you, and you do not have to deal with the pages flapping in the wind. Creating a space outside to tell stories in is also a help, as suggested in the activity above. Figure 3.1 is one of my favourite pictures, and is of a storytelling space created for me, seen here in the snow. It is a hidden space in the summer, as the leaf canopy screens it almost entirely, and there is only one path in through the briars. There is a circle of logs to sit or lean on, with a slightly larger one for the storyteller, and the atmosphere is still and attentive, waiting for the story. Once you get started, the Society for Storytellers (www.sfs.org.uk) has resources and ideas that can help you get started.

Kites, flags and others

Many stories about kites are of Japanese origin. And another way to see the air is to fly a kite and see the wind lift and carry it along. Kites come in all complexities and sizes, and in the UK the Kite Society has festivals where they can be flown together. You will also find health and safety guidance on their website (www.thekitesociety.org.uk) about when and where to fly kites. There are kite designs, too, although simpler ones suitable for preschool children to try can be found on www. blueskylark.org/zoo. The activity below shows the simplest starting point for kite making. There is rarely enough space in the outdoor spaces of settings to fly kites, so creating these will make a good reason

Figure 3.1   Storytelling in the snow

for an expedition to an open, wilder space where the children can try flying their kites.

 ## Activity: simple kites

Children can decorate a slightly elongated diamond shape and stick drinking straws on it as cross-braces. If the kites are to fly, they will need a tail to weight them down, longer than the kite itself and also decorated. If you are going to fly them, you will need to tie the string to the centre of the cross-bracing, or you can hang them as banners from their tops.

Flags and banners are also good ways to see the wind, and can inspire much discussion about their purposes and meanings. Babies are always attracted by movement, and this can be provided by flags moving in the breeze. Settings may like to design their own flags to fly. These can be useful when setting up camps in wilder spaces or on beaches, as the children can quickly locate their base camp if they can see a flag. Older children may be interested in the Buddhist uses of prayer flags, which are traditionally tied to bamboo poles.

There are an increasing number of wind turbines in the landscape, which demonstrate the power of the wind to create electricity. They are huge, and by comparison children's handheld windmills are very small, but they will also turn in the wind. When out walking, children can 'collect' images of windmills on camera, including grinding mills and pumping mills. Windmill World at www.windmillworld.com is an excellent resource if mills become a favourite thing to look for with your children. If you decide to explore a mill, it is wise to make a preliminary visit to assess the hazards and risks so that you can work out the ratios of adults to children appropriate to your children.

Weathervanes indicate wind direction, and can be artistic creations as well. Good examples can be seen on www.windgallery.nl. Spotting these when out walking can prompt discussions on the points of the compass, which in turn heightens children's awareness of the direction of the sun as well as of the wind. This links to ideas about shadows described below.

Light and dark and in-between

Light and dark are obvious qualities of air. Children will be more familiar with light than with dark, but there are ways to explore both. When considering light, there are ways that we can raise children's awareness of natural light and its power. This is important as we ourselves develop our understanding of the damage that can be caused by sunburn. Shading children from the sun is an important task for practitioners, and it is made easier if those children are developing an understanding of its power.

Even before such awareness can enter the child's conscious mind, it is important that babies and toddlers can experience the air around them. Parking prams under trees provides babies with the natural 'mobile' of moving branches and leaves, and they will be able to become aware of the differences of light and shade. As they grow older, tasks like shading seedlings to prevent scorching, and drying dollies' clothes in the sun may provide incidental opportunities that help children to develop their understanding. When children think about their environment in naturally occurring ways, they become better attuned to it.

Shadows are fascinating phenomena that children will notice, and if their attention to them is encouraged by discussion, the shadows will help the children to develop their understanding of the sun. Observing and playing with shadows will help them to explore ideas about light sources, and links to thoughts about the direction of the sun as mentioned above. Being aware of where the sun is in the sky is important when in wilder spaces. It helps to decide where to locate shelters, dens and tents. The best orientation will depend on a number of factors, but knowing that south is where the sun is in the middle part of the day for most of the year (in the northern hemisphere), and being able to locate it, is a useful and simple skill. Getting children into the habit of thinking about this will stand them in good stead if they progress to exploring wilder places when they are older.

Rainbows are sources of awe and wonder, prompting stories and discussions. In my nursery, we had two prisms that would split the light in the same way as the sun refracting through rain to create rainbows, which the children found fascinating to play with. Memories of such activities will help stimulate study in later years. Settings can explore the colours of the rainbow in many ways, for example by painting their fences in the correct sequence of rainbow stripes.

The only risk associated with light has to be that from looking directly at the sun, but there are real emotional risks in engaging with the dark. In the winter, children may well arrive at or leave settings in the dark, so there are opportunities to explore the quality of darkness. In towns and cities, light pollution means that children rarely get a good look at the night sky, so if the opportunity does arise when children are out and about, it should be seized upon. Just as lying on your back looking at clouds and the tracery of branches can stimulate the imagination, so too can looking at the night sky, particularly on a starry night.

Once children have developed their walking skills, giving them the opportunity to be out in the dark is a good experience. Even where there are no street lamps, they will find that there is some light around, usually starlight and moonlight, and that their eyes will adjust sufficiently to allow them to move around safely. Locating an ideal spot is clearly going to involve considering safety issues, but in the UK the Forestry Commission, wildlife trusts and environmental centres do organise walks to explore the dark, so contacting them may open up an opportunity to visit places only usually seen in daylight. A winter walk in the dark can help them to learn to navigate uneven surfaces with different cues to those used on a daytime walk. With older children, it is fun to do a simple orientation exercise around your own outdoor area, finding places or things as part of a game or competition.

Many children are frightened of the dark so being out after dark can prompt discussions about darkness and why it can feel scary. Storybooks can help explore the scariness of the dark, and make the fear manageable by putting it into words. There is a good evolutionary reason why we have an instinctive fear of the dark, being essentially a vulnerable species with poor night vision and inadequate escape mechanisms, and some overcome that instinct quicker than others. For this reason, children may be nervous of entering thick woodland in summer because it seems dark by contrast to the space outside. It is good to unpick the idea that some dark places can seem scary if they are unknown, and how best to deal with that. Holding hands is a comfort to all of us, as it is to know how to find your way around by following signs and tracks left by animals, helpful adults or by the children themselves if this is a return visit. I will consider tracks in more depth in Chapter 6.

In the last chapter, I described the specialness of in-between places like beaches, and dusk or dawn, the in-between day and night times. If children are in your settings long enough to experience the dark, they will also be there as darkness falls or as the sun comes up. Often there are fleeting moments of dramatic colour as well as times when colours fade or build slowly. If you can create a quiet place where children can experience these transitions if they wish to, they will be able to tap into their creativity and may produce special stories, poems and pictures that capture the colours and the spirit of those times. The storytelling space you are creating may well be the right place for this to happen, and sitting wrapped up together to stay warm, quietly watching the world change, can be a magical experience.

Sounds of the air

Having dealt with some ways in which children can be encouraged to 'see' the air, I will now consider ways in which they might 'hear' it. I would hope that practitioners will encourage children to listen to the wind, whether they hear it when they are indoors or out, but these opportunities may be far apart for some children, so I will talk about things we can do to make the sounds more accessible. Once again, I will be thinking about second-hand air, in other words the sounds that air causes to be made, rather than the pure sounds of rushing air. I will concentrate first on the wilder sounds, the sounds that untamed air makes, rather than the air mediated by our inhalation and exhalation.

Aeolus was the god of the winds in ancient Greek mythology, and Aeolian harps have been popular throughout history. These are musical instruments that make noises when the wind blows over and through them. In 1809, Turner painted a picture called 'Thomson's Aeolian Harp', depicting one such instrument set in a rural landscape. A modern Aeolian harp is being developed at the time of writing by artist Luke Jerram, who is working with schools on this project, as can be seen from a visit to his website: www.lukejerram.com/projects/aelous_acoustic_wind_pavillion. Another has been installed at the Cornwall Harp Centre, and again there are pictures on their website: www.cornwallharpcentre shop.co.uk. Children will be fascinated by hollow pipes and stretched strings that create sound in the wind, but this is an unusual concept. They may need to play with pan pipes and recorders before moving to experimenting with hollow tubes and pipes to blow across to develop this idea. Another alternative is co-creating sculptures that make sounds, as can be seen in the following activity.

 ### Activity: creating an Aeolian instrument from found objects

Collect hollow wood, bamboo or old metal pipes to create your sculpture, and use wires in place of strings, as they are less likely to deteriorate in the weather. Locate a windy spot in your outdoor setting, perhaps where a draft is created between two buildings. Work with the children to arrange the objects in a pleasing shape, with openings and hollow tops outwards. It may resemble a harp, an organ or a creation of their choosing. Joining them up can be permanent or temporary. You can tie them with string or wire to create a temporary structure that you can change and experiment with, or you can set it in concrete. Old plastic buckets or large tins are good for this, and use a small bag of ready mixed concrete from your local DIY store. This will give the children experience of a different medium, but encourage them to wear gloves and use spades, and do wash splashes off skin thoroughly, as it is slightly caustic. If the shape is very irregular, you will need to support it while the concrete sets, but that is only a matter of hours.

Figure 3.2 is a wind sculpture I created from old organ pipes – it now quietly hums and taps rather than making the glory of its previous sounds. The angles are achieved by setting the pipes into an old paint pot full of concrete and propping them up until set; it would not have been safe to make this as a temporary structure, due to the weight. Having used concrete, moving it into its final resting place took the efforts of several people and a wheelbarrow.

Easier for children to create are wind chimes, which can be made from a wide variety of found objects. Brighter sounds come from joining sections of pipe together, with quieter and more natural sounds from lengths of wood. The activity below explores a way to make natural wind chimes which can be done in the setting or in a wilder location, and if all the materials used are biodegradable, they can be left hanging in trees until they disappear naturally over time. Earthenware flowerpots make excellent bells and plastic ones can be used for chimes, as you can make holes around the edges from which to suspend the chiming objects.

Figure 3.2 Organ pipe sculpture

 Activity: wild wood wind chimes with string and sticks

Select a stick to be the hanger, and tie a string to either end. While the children are making the chimes, they can hang this from a low branch. Ask them to select items that make a sound when they are tapped together. Hollow objects will make louder sounds. Tie a string to each and suspend them from the stick close together and at the same height – it will depend on the age and experience of your children as to how much of the tying they can manage. Now they can suspend their creations where they like, and listen to the sounds they make when the wind blows on them.

It is the air in hollow objects which amplifies the sound, the space allowing the sound waves to move and carry sound to our ears. Fallen wood in different stages of decay has different amounts of airspaces, and therefore makes different sounds. Children enjoy tapping logs with sticks to discover their sound, and my groups and I have often evolved into a gamelan-style band as we create rhythmic sound patterns in the woods. This can be a noisy adventure into sound, but worth exploring as these are the kinds of activities it is so hard to do indoors. The two necessary elements, sticks and loud noises, are two that practitioners find it hard to cope with indoors, but outside there is enough space to swing a stick safely, and enough space to accommodate the loudest banging.

Points for practice

The ideas in this chapter have not involved what we conventionally think of as risk and adventure, but they have both been present. From storytelling to creating sculptures that make sounds, I have described activities that could involve emotional risks. Risk is relative to the person experiencing it, and emotional risks are as real as physical ones, with equally dangerous outcomes. If practitioners mishandle a child's fear of the dark, the results can be as long-term as a physical accident. Similarly, adventures in creativity can be brought to an abrupt end if adults quash children's enthusiasms and expressive output. The risks can be those taken by the practitioners, too, in allowing their 'control' to slip as activities become more child-led. In good practice, practitioners will be working to develop a positive environment where these social and emotional risks and adventures can be safely explored (Eaude, 2008). It is possible to prevent emotional mistakes occurring if practitioners are well-trained in child development, know their children and are sensitive to the potential issues.

The first professional need, to be well-trained, can be addressed through a robust programme of Continual Professional Development. Courses can include in-house activities. For example, settings could establish a reading rota so that each month a member of staff takes on the task of reading something new, either a book, paper or article, and then telling the rest of the staff about it and its implications for practice. In this way, there is a method for staying up-to-date with current ideas about child development and a process for valuing the input from all staff members. Outdoor skills can be gained in a variety of ways. In the UK, Forest School practitioner awards are available from vocational level (VQ) 1 to VQ level 4, a managerial award. These will often include support to gain first-aid qualifications suitable for working with children in wilder areas away from easy sources of support. In addition, they include tool use and knowledge about the environment. To find out about courses in your area, contact one of the organisations listed in Appendix 1. Local wildlife trusts, outdoor centres and environmental centres can offer useful short courses such as identifying fungi, tracks, animal calls, etc. The additional benefit of these is that they will be relevant to the environments available in particular areas.

The second professional need, to know the children, has been addressed in the EYFS, with the guidance towards a key worker system (Principles into Practice 2.4) and recording learning journeys (Principles into Practice 3.2). This builds on the work of Margaret Carr in using learning stories not just to record but also to plan children's learning experiences based on their interests and excitement (Carr, 2001). Sharing these between practitioners and engaging with the children and their families in their development can enrich practitioners' knowledge and understanding of each child.

The third professional need, to be sensitive and empathetic, is clearly a skill that we would hope to find in all early years practitioners, but one that comes more easily to some than others. This ability can only be developed in environments where practitioners feel empowered and positive about their work, as explained by Stacey (2009). This is a part of the managerial role, to inspire and empower (Canning, 2009), not easy in the UK where early years practitioners are still often under-qualified and poorly paid. The two books referenced here offer creative ideas to managers in their endeavours to develop their teams.

 Discussion points

Think about your own storytelling skills:

- What would help you to develop your ability to tell stories without a book?
- Is there a space in your outdoor area where you could tell stories?
- Can you decorate it with a wind chime or Aeolian instrument?

Further reading

Duffy, B. (2006) *Supporting Creativity and Imagination in the Early Years*. Maidenhead: Open University Press.

Maynard, T. (2007) 'Encounters with Forest School and Foucault: a risky business?', *Education 3–13*, 35 (4): 379–91.

Robins, A. and Callan, S. (2009) *Managing Early Years Settings*. London: Sage.

Fire

Chapter objectives

In this chapter, I aim to:

- consider the importance of fire in outdoor experiences
- explore ways to enable young children to experience fire
- discuss appropriate settings for fire
- look at topics related to fire.

Introduction

In this chapter I will discuss the fourth element, fire. As with the other elements, it attracts and fascinates us at all ages, which is why it is essential to learn about it. It, too, has the power to create and the power to destroy, which is why it has a part in our learning about outdoor adventures and risks. And, as with the other three elements, we can never gain complete control over it, only learn to respect it so that we can use and direct it. Without this knowledge, we may be fearful without knowing how to control it and how to keep ourselves safe, as can be seen in the case study below.

 Case study: fire with three-year-old child A

I had worked with an early years class, taking them to a local wood for Forest School sessions over a period of six weeks. Over that time, I had slowly built up the children's knowledge and experience so that I could light a small fire with them. The day came

(Continued)

(Continued)

when we were to do this, and to cook our snack. The children collected the wood, and watched as I lit the fire, a small affair some 15 centimetres cubed at most. To my surprise, one child burst into tears as the fire took hold, and turned to an assistant for comfort. The situation was managed, and the activity continued, with the child calm but relying on the assistant for support. On our return to the setting, I drew the adult team together for a debriefing, and looked to the child's key worker, who explained that the child had an older sibling who had been burned, seriously but not with lasting injuries, by a bonfire, and subsequently the family had avoided all contact with fire. The child had learned a fear of fire rather than a respect for it, understandable in the circumstances but one it would have been helpful to be aware of in advance of the activity. We would then have been able to help the child to be prepared to meet his fear, and had the appropriate support in place before it became necessary. As it is, through his subsequent Forest School sessions, he was able to learn how to keep himself safe and thus avoid the danger his brother had faced.

When I am giving talks to early years groups in the UK and I want to gain immediate attention, I introduce myself as the lady who lights fires with three-year-olds. Not by setting light to them, I add hastily, which always gets a smile. Why should this be such an attention-grabbing start? In other parts of the world, lighting a campfire is a natural accompaniment to a visit to wilder places with any age group. It is an important part of establishing a camp, whether that is for a lunch break or for an overnight stop. One reason may be because our island is so crowded, so that for many it is unusual to be so far from civilisation that they need the safety of a fire, and unusual to have the space to safely light a fire. Because of this we have ceased to think of the safety of a fire, and tend only to think of the danger of fire.

However, as we become more aware of the importance of outdoor experiences to our quality of life, so we are becoming more aware of the benefits of activities such as lighting fires. The Forestry Commission now provides opportunities to learn to light fires safely, and provides areas where it is safe to do so (for an example, see Forestry Commission Press Release 12620, 2 July 2009). The Woodland Trust goes so far as to include a recipe for soup to cook over your campfire (see www.woodlandtrust. org.uk/en/our-woods/visiting/things-to-do/pages/wildfoodrecipes.aspx) and both the Scouting Movement and Woodcraft Folk have returned to their use of campfires for cooking and socialising after a blip at the end of the last century.

In this chapter, I will look at the route to the safe use of fire with young children. I would also recommend Danks and Schofield's book, listed at the end of the chapter, for even more detailed guidance, or the Scouts fact sheet FS315076 downloadable from: www.scoutbase.org.uk/ library/hqdocs/facts/. Fire safety is largely about using common sense and gaining confidence, and it will enhance your outdoor learning to include the opportunity for the children to gain safe confidence around fire. Wrangham (2009) states that it was the discovery of fire that enabled our pre-human ancestors to develop into homo sapiens, which underlines its importance to us and our place on the planet.

Pre-fire activities

The level of children's engagement with fire will clearly depend upon their age and stage of development, and the amount of prior experience they have of fire. In the UK, most families do not have a tradition of having lighted candles and tea lights around indoors, which means that very young children do not grow up absorbing adult behaviour around flames in the house. Birthdays and Christmases are likely to be children's first encounters with candles, setting in their minds the idea that candles are for special times and are exciting. Similarly, few houses have open fires to accustom children to being routinely aware of spitting logs or hot coals. With gardens becoming smaller, even bonfires to burn rubbish are less familiar. Most of the cultural acclimatisation has disappeared, so children will be relying on the adults who first take them out to a campfire to set the boundaries and establish the routines.

Giving children below the age of three with limited or no prior experience access to fire will require close attention and 1:1 ratios, and their level of activity is likely to be limited to watching the flames and to benefiting from the output of any cooking activities, neither of which are unattractive or wasted occupations. Even at this level of contact, they are learning valuable lessons about adult respect for fire and about the uses fire can be put to. If they do not have such simple opportunities, then they are more likely to be both foolish and fearful when they do encounter fire.

With children of three or above, it is possible to involve them more fully in creating a campfire suitable for cooking or as a focal point for a camp. As our children are so unused to being around open fires however, it is a good idea to facilitate activities that will start them thinking about fires in constructive ways before reaching this point. Role play is a powerful tool, and I have found that many children will spontaneously arrange sticks to make a pretend fire as soon as they are established playing in a wild area. The sensitive interventions of adults should be around drawing out the following themes:

1 Fires need to be positioned carefully, where they will not spread to overhanging materials and are not on a thoroughfare.
2 They will burn whatever they are set on, so (for example) grass should be protected by lifting a turf.
3 Materials to be burned need to be dry.
4 When the materials are collected, they are stacked to one side before feeding the fire.
5 Cooking fires are small.
6 Only the cook feeds the fire.
7 Kettles and pots can be placed on the fire or suspended above it.
8 Cooking utensils have long handles to protect the hands and arms.
9 Fires must be kept small in order to be manageable.
10 Fires must be thoroughly put out before being left.

These are points that I will return to as they are dealt with in relation to the real thing. The following activity suggests starting points for one such role-play activity.

Alongside opportunities for role play, practitioners will need to casually start to feed in the idea that a campfire would be a nice event, giving the opportunity for cooking a snack. In this way, it is possible to set up the expectation that this will happen when the adults are sure that everyone understands how to behave around fire, and can follow the safety rules around the campfire area. It is preferable that this is done without it becoming a negative pressure on the children, and just a simple statement of the facts. It is important that practitioners and children alike are comfortable with the idea, and that the level of anticipation is positive rather than excited, as it is when feelings are running too high that accidents can occur.

 ## Activity: starting a role play about making a campfire

Whilst it is not desirable to prescribe a role-play event, children can be stimulated by adult ideas, and sensitive adults can make valuable inputs to role play. When settling to play in a wilder space, children will enjoy claiming an area for their own camp, which can become an outdoor version of a 'home corner'. It may involve making a den, an activity in its own right described later in the book, or just the identification of an area they feel ownership of. This can be the stimulus to setting up a cooking fire. Another stimulus might be by an adult building their own imaginary fire in an adjacent area. Or it might be that the play has included pretend 'fishing' with twigs, and the catch will then need cooking for tea. These have all worked with groups that I have taken outside. As the play progresses, the cues to feed in the points stated above will arise. On subsequent occasions, observing adults will be able to see if the children have absorbed the information by their rehearsal of the key points in their play.

In the wrong hands fires can be dangerous, so it is important that practitioners only progress to lighting fires with children when they feel that they have sufficient expertise and when they feel that the children are ready for this step. Clearly, training and experience are key factors to successful campfires. This may seem over-prescriptive to readers from outside the UK, but we have been through a period of over ten years when campfire activities were not the norm, and the underlying general level of knowledge about fire management has dropped. It is for this reason that I make the recommendations above. I still believe that it is a desirable outcome to aim for, helping our children to establish good habits of outdoor experiences. Fires create a sense of security and companionship at a very basic level of our humanity, and children should not be excluded from safely experiencing that warm glow.

Establishing a location for a fire

The first requirement for a fire is the permission of the landowner. For example, the Forestry Commission have rules about where and how fires may be lit on their land, largely to reduce the risk of forest fires. If a landowner refuses permission for a campfire, you must respect their wishes, and in addition you may find it a useful reflection to consider their reasons, a process that could develop your own understanding of their environment. You may be able to use one of the alternative methods of cooking discussed below, and so still cook a snack, which is a valuable sharing experience.

The idea of any camp and fire is that you will be able to leave the space as you found it, with no trace of your visit. Clearly, if you are using the same space for a period of months this will be much harder to achieve than after a one-day event, but that is the ultimate goal. When choosing your site, remember that it is easier for grass to regrow than to erase the kinds of marks from rock that archaeologists use today to locate Stone Age fireplaces from thousands of years ago.

If you are establishing a site that you will return to, and that you are using with a moderately sized group, your needs will be different to that of a one-off stop on an outing, or the building of a permanent site in your outdoor area. I will be describing the needs for the first of these, and lessons for the other two can be deduced from that. The first consideration is a big enough space to set out logs to sit on, that are placed a sufficient distance from the fire so that little toes will not scorch even when stretched out. The central point, the fireplace itself, needs to avoid vegetation below and above. If you are on grass, you should cut out a patch of turf and save it to replace when you leave, and if this will be after some time you should water it, roll it up and keep it in a shady spot. If you are under trees, be sure that no branches are directly above the fire space. Your fire area should be far enough away from shelters so that sparks cannot fly in the wind towards them, and not be on a main thoroughfare through the camp. Your fire will need a draft, but should also be in the lee of the prevailing wind.

Avoid lighting fires on rocks. Apart from the scorching mentioned above, there is a slight danger that heated stones will explode.

Establishing the seating logs is a good way to start preparing the children to respect the space. You can create a square or a triangle or two parallel lines, but the idea is to enclose and define the space designated as the fire area. It is a good idea to peg the logs in place by hammering short pieces of wood on either side and at either end. This will stop them rolling or being shunted towards the fire. If you can maintain an access path behind them, you can also maintain the good rule that children should approach their seats from behind, stepping over the log and then sitting down on them. This stops them from crossing the fire area at all, which is a good safety precaution. If you cannot define your area with logs, you can lay a circle of chain on the ground to show the children the area where it is unsafe to walk when the fire is lit.

If you wish, you can define the central spot where the fire will be lit by laying a pair of wet or green logs in parallel, on either side of where the fire will be. You do not want these to burn as a part of the fire, but they can be useful for helping to balance a kettle. It is not essential, however. Your fire does not have to be big to be effective; the one shown in Figure 4.1 is at the larger end of the spectrum needed for heating a kettle. Fires can be made in a variety of ways equally successfully, depending on your circumstances. Laying your fire on clear bare earth is the basic starting point. If it is very wet, you can construct a raft of green sticks; if it is very windy, hollow out a slight trough (but ensure you still have a draft).

All of the above procedures can be undertaken as you work towards your fire lighting event. You do not need to rush, but do need to consolidate each part of the construction process with your children until you all feel comfortable and familiar with the site, and are confident that you all not only know the rules but comply with them without thinking about it. If you are working with a group of children who are under five years old and who have limited or no experience of campfires, this process can take four or five weeks. It is all a part of learning about the value and pleasure of having a campfire.

Fire lighting

When you are ready to light your fire with the children, do ensure that you have a full water container (at least a gallon) with you for when you

Figure 4.1 Making tea

need to put it out. Fires need air to burn, and water is the quickest way to eliminate the supply of air. It probably will not be sufficient, and you will need to cover the fire with earth as well, but that can be a part of the digging-in process to ensure that you cover your tracks. The activity below describes the preparatory process for collecting the materials you will need for a successful fire.

 ## Activity: engaging the children in collecting material to burn

The first material you will need to start your fire will be tinder, and it may be advisable to bring your own in a sealed container, to ensure success. The ultimate cheat is a couple of cotton wool balls with just a light smear of Vaseline – they will need to be teased out to let the air through. However, do send the children to look for the driest materials to make natural tinder, such as dead (dry) grass and leaves, the fluffy seeds from rosebay willowherb and wild clematis. If you are in a hazel wood, you may find 'King Alfred's Cakes', a hard black fungus stuck to the trees, which is like charcoal to burn. Next you will need kindling, usually thin dead wood. The best dead wood is that which is 'hanging', i.e. caught up in other vegetation above ground level, as there it will be at its driest. Make separate piles beside the fire site of the different sizes. Start with twigs that

(Continued)

(Continued)

are as thin as a match and as long as the children's hands. Describing the wood to collect in these terms helps the children to sort by suitable size, as you can show them what you mean. Next you need twigs as thick as the children's little fingers and as long as their forearms. Ask them to test the wood by snapping it – it is only dry enough if it snaps easily and cleanly. Lastly, you will need fuel, which is thicker wood. The children may become very enthusiastic at this stage, and find long pieces of dead branches that they struggle to drag back to camp, which will give you the opportunity to demonstrate the use of suitable tools to cut them into useable sizes. This wood will need to be dry to start with, but a well-established fire will burn greener wood, although that will create more smoke. Keep your fuel stacked to one side and do not feed the fire with more than you need, or it will be difficult to put out.

When you have all your material together, you can light the fire. You can light it with a match, in which case do store the matchbox in a sealed container – if you keep it with your tinder, you have your kit all together. Damp matches, like damp tinder, can ruin a good plan. There are other methods which are not susceptible to damp, but which tend to need more skill, such as a striker or flint, or methods that are reminiscent of older times, such as friction methods and the use of lenses, but these are challenges that will be enjoyed by older children or in more adventurous settings.

Build a tiny tipi of kindling over a nest of tinder, and hold the match close to the tinder. Ensure that the tinder has lit the kindling before you start to add more material. Build your fire slowly, allowing the air to circulate through the middle, until the fuel has caught properly. Do not try to cook until you have a good bed of embers. You will need patience, and this will be difficult for the children, too. This is when the weeks of pre-fire activities pay off, as they will know that only the cook feeds the fire (point 6 above), and that in this case that person is a practitioner. You can engage them in peeling sticks to cook their snack on, while the fire becomes established.

Below are some suggestions for snacks to prepare. Once you have finished with your fire, you will need to allow sufficient time to ensure that it has gone out before you leave the area. Hopefully it will have died right down before you start this process, or it will be a more difficult task, as fire is persistent in thick wood even after the outer layers have been soaked. Pour water over the fire, then cover it with earth, and then dig the ashes in, even if you intend to reuse the area the following week.

Figure 4.2 The author lighting a fire with three-year-olds

When you have finished with the area completely, you will need to reinstate it to its original form – remove the logs, cover all traces and replace the grass if necessary.

Alternatives to campfires

If you are going to include fires in your settings, you may prefer to contain them in some way, as this is less likely to cause damage to plant material. You can buy fire boxes, fire pans and fire buckets, but you can also create your own. A metal biscuit tin will contain your fire, and can be sunk into the ground or stood on a brick platform. The former is more stable and therefore safer; the latter causes less damage to your garden. Metal hubcaps can be cradled in a brick nest to create a fire pan, which are good for small fires but not so good for boiling kettles.

If your main purpose is to cook then a BBQ is efficient, but does not engage the children in the same way. If your fire has a social focus then a fire pan is better. Figure 4.3 shows a large fire pan in front of an even larger fire pit, and you can see that the pan is a more contained shape. On expeditions, the quickest and most efficient way to heat water for a drink or soup is to use a storm kettle (also called kelly kettles, ghillie kettles and volcano kettles), which is constructed of concentric tubes of metal with the fire in the centre, but it is not interesting for the children nor easy to operate until they are older. Other methods of cooking

Figure 4.3   Bishops Wood fire bowl and pit

outside include burying food in various ways and piling fire on or around it, but these involve bushcraft skills which are more appropriate for older children or adults.

Food and drink

Food tastes better outside. In the summer, you may be able to eat outside at your setting, which will give you your usual resources to draw on. But you may also wish to cook outside, particularly if you are growing things to eat and can show the children the path from plant to plate in one activity. Consider making soup in a pot on a fire or BBQ outside from your vegetables, as well as making kebabs to toast, or eating them raw.

When planning to cook outside and in the wild, there are things to consider. Obviously, you will have to carry everything with you, so simplicity is good. Also, you are going to bring out any rubbish you take in, so packaging needs to be kept to a minimum. With young children, a quick result is preferable, but you also need to think about dietary issues. This creates an instant dilemma, as toasting marshmallows is great fun, easy and involves very little rubbish. It is also an opportunity for their first lesson in tool use, to peel the end of a stick suitable for sticking a marshmallow onto. If you succumb to this temptation, your children will need thin green sticks from a non-poisonous source such as hazel, cut about a metre long with the tip peeled (see the following activity). The marshmallows will cook quickly, the outsides crisping and changing colour. The insides become soft and gooey. Being sugar, they are very hot in the middle, so children need to count five elephants (saying the word elephant takes about one second) before eating them.

 ## Activity: peeling sticks

Whilst all outdoor practitioners working with young children agree that sharp tools are safer than blunt ones, or 'toy' ones which do not do the job they claim to do, there is a debate about the best way to introduce children to using sharp tools in the woods. Some prefer to introduce the techniques of stick peeling with a knife, the tool designed for the job, while others prefer to start with a potato peeler, arguing that although the tool is designed to peel vegetables not sticks, the blade is less dangerous than a knife until the techniques have been acquired. Whichever tool you use, the technique for peeling a stick is the same, and establishes a safe ritual for later tool use. The stick is selected, and a place identified where the child can quietly peel it. The tool is collected once this has been done, so that the child is not wandering around with the tool in their hand. Ensure that the child is sitting or kneeling to use the tool, and that they work along the stick in the direction away from the body, and pointing towards the ground. Turn the stick as it is peeled, rather than the tool. Put the tool down in an agreed safe place when the task is complete. Tools should be stored under supervision and counted in and out.

Popcorn is not as sinful, provided you do not add sugar or salt, and also cooks quickly. Wire together two metal sieves, and bind the handles to a thicker stick to create a mobile corn popper. Do not put too much corn into the popper at a time.

Medium-length cooking is required for baking bananas in their skins, but as these are best wrapped in foil you will need to take the dirty foil wraps home with you to be recycled, and you may need spoons to eat them with – another complication. However, they are nutritious and healthy, unlike the dampers that I made as a Girl Guide. We made a simple flour and water dough and stuck lumps of it onto our sticks (thicker than those needed for marshmallows). When toasted they were pulled off the sticks and filled with jam. But then, active children do need carbohydrates to keep them going!

Kebabs are another medium-length cooking item, but most other food will need longer. For example, baked potatoes are popular but require a couple of hours to be edible. Therefore, unless you have planned a long stay, it is better to stick to simple snacks.

Drinks are much quicker. The storm kettle mentioned above will heat two litres of water in three minutes once lit. In the winter when it is cold, it is comforting to have a hot drink when you are outside for any length of time. Hot fruit drinks such as blackcurrant are refreshing and easy, as the water does not have to boil and there is no need for milk.

It is worth experimenting to find the best compromise for you and your children. It may be that your wild fires are just for fun, and your outdoor cooking takes place in the outdoor space at your setting.

 Points for practice

With the groups of three-year-olds I have taken out, I have been lucky to have had a relationship of mutual trust with the practitioners concerned, and have always felt able to light fires when I have wanted to. It is only when I talk to them afterwards that they confess to nervousness on the first occasion. If they had not been with a more experienced practitioner, they would not have made that step, and their children would have missed out. It is therefore a helpful move to link with other groups and find a more confident person to help with that first fire-lighting session.

To find a like-minded group, look on the Forest Education Initiative website for your nearest Forest School cluster group. They will be able to put you in touch with practitioners confident in lighting campfires. Similarly, your local Scouts, Guides or Woodcraft folk should be familiar with lighting fires in the company of children, and may be happy to undertake activities together.

If campfires become a more normal event for children then they will gain in confidence around fire, and are less likely to be foolish or fearful in later years. They will be more likely to respect fire, being aware of what it can do, whether that is in the home or in wilder places. In this way, we will be less likely to see out-of-control fires, and children getting burned.

 Discussion points

Consider whether you could light a fire in your outdoor space:

- Would your storytelling area accommodate a fire pan?
- Could you have a BBQ lunch in the summer?
- Could you cook soup over a campfire in the winter?
- Can you think of alternative snacks to cook over an open fire?

Further reading 📖

Callaway, G. (2005) *The Early Years Curriculum: A View From Outdoors*. London: David Fulton.

Danks, F. and Schofield, J. (2009) *Go Wild: 101 Things To Do Before You Grow Up*. London: Frances Lincoln.

Hope, G., Austin, R., Dismore, H., Hammond, S. and Whyte, T. (2007) 'Wild woods or urban jungle: playing it safe or freedom to roam', *Education 3–13*, 35 (4): 321–32.

5

Seasonal Changes

Chapter objectives

In this chapter, I aim to:

- encourage practitioners to be aware of the rhythms in nature
- think about linking outdoor activities to healthy eating
- discuss gardening and harvesting opportunities for pre-school settings
- consider the seasonal adventures available to practitioners and their children.

Introduction

In the UK, we are fortunate in having four distinct seasons, none of which are too extreme. This double bonus means that we can help our children to develop an awareness of the adventure of change and of the natural rhythms of living things without too much risk and danger. The children may need sunscreen in the summer, waterproofs in spring and autumn and woolly jumpers in the winter, but rarely do they need to stay indoors to escape violent extremes of temperature or precipitation. In this chapter, I will use each of the UK seasons in turn to suggest ways of engaging your children with their world in ways that will help them to feel in harmony with nature.

The disadvantage of our weather is that our seasons tend to merge at the edges, so practitioners will need to watch their world rather than read the books when deciding where we are in any one year. Observation is a key to this chapter, of nature and of children, and the flexibility to react to such observations that comes from being comfortable in your environment. We will consider seasonal change and discuss ways to facilitate children's links with the natural rhythm of the seasons. This will lead to opportunities for growing things, such as vegetables and flowers. In turn this links with fostering good eating habits, and thus helping to counter obesity, which is often a popular link to outdoor work for practitioners. In each section, I will discuss the importance of observing changes from leaf burst to leaf fall, and how to record and reuse leaves, primroses, catkins, etc., opening up opportunities for poetry and storytelling.

Ways to grow fruits, to compost, to nurture and to harvest are skills that we as a culture risk losing as we become increasingly dependent on supermarkets for our food; this is an important risk to counter. You will need to think about who and how to ask for support if you do not feel confident or need extra pairs of hands. Parents and grandparents may like to engage with gardening activities, and environmental experts may be able to help with ideas for harvesting the bounty of the wilder places. This seasonal play can link the wilder areas of the outdoor environment to your gardening areas.

Winter

This is one of the best times to be outside, when everything is stripped down to its basic forms. There are no leaves to blur the shapes of the trees or hide the colours of the earth. It is cold, so there is a need to stay active and be doing things. With a clear palette, it is a good time for planning, looking forward to the growing season to come.

Things to do

Now is a good time to engage your children in planning for the year ahead. Decide where in your setting you can grow things, and prepare the area if that is possible. Two things may stop you – concrete and clay. If your setting has only paved areas, your growing may be restricted to gro-bags, planters and baskets, but these still offer plenty of opportunities, as can be seen in the array from the Chelsea Open Air Day Nursery School in Figure 5.1. If the soil you do have is heavy clay then walking on it in winter will not improve its condition, and you may want to consider a raised bed instead.

Alongside preparing your garden, the children can be engaged in feeding the birds. Different kinds of food attract different visitors. For example, the black thistle seeds will attract goldfinches, which are so pretty. You will need the right feeder for the right food. The most expensive is likely to be for the peanuts, as this will have to be squirrel-proof and thus very sturdy. A cage put over ground-level feed will help keep off pigeons and other larger visitors. Putting the food out first thing in the morning and

Figure 5.1   Pots and planters at Chelsea Open Air Nursery School

taking in any leftovers in the evening will help deter rats. The next activity gives some ideas for hanging feeders that the children can make to attract tits, robins and other small birds.

Winter walks and opportunities to experience the dark have been discussed before, as has dealing with ice and snow, although I did not mention snowmen and snow angels, both important contributions to winter play when available. Snowmen are best made when the snow is not too cold, so that it will stick together, but falling backwards into the snow and waving your arms and legs up and down to make snow angels can be done in any snow covering.

Things to eat

In this section, I will be considering the food that is available seasonally, some of it from the wild, as well as the needs of the children. When it is cold, there is a need for food that is robust and solid, and fortunately this is the season for root vegetables, which can be roasted or made into soup. Roasting them wrapped in foil on the campfire or on kebabs is tasty, but takes time. Soup can be made out of anything, so experimenting with the help of the children is a good activity. You can make the soup outside or indoors and heat it up on your campfire, or take it out on your walks in thermos flasks. It is nourishing, warming and satisfying. If you make it with fresh, and preferably local, vegetables with just stock to dilute it, it will be packed with goodness and natural carbohydrates that will benefit the children. My favourites are potatoes and herbs, parsnips with curry, or turnips, which need no accompanying flavours. When they are boiled to a softness, you can liquidise or mash them to give a smoother texture and a thicker soup. If you have had a glut of any produce in the summer, you may have your own frozen produce that you can also use.

 ## Activity: wild bird food

Each person can find their own container for their bird food mix to be put in. Suggestions include a yoghurt pot, a log with holes in, a juice container with the sides cut out to leave a six-centimetre tray or half a coconut shell. Consider how they will hang up, and help the children to add strings as needed. For example, make a small hole in the bottom of the yoghurt pot, push some string through from the bottom and knot it on the inside to stop it pulling out. Gently melt some vegetable or beef fat in a saucepan. Ask the children to add in seeds, chopped nuts, raisins, apple pieces or vegetable scraps. Allow the mix to set a little, and then pour it into the containers. Put them in the fridge to set hard. Hang them outdoors for the birds to enjoy. You can even turn out those that are in yoghurt pots to make bell-shaped hangings.

Things to observe

Many creatures slow down or sleep through the winter, so encouraging children to watch for likely hibernation sites and to take care not to disturb the inhabitants will help them to tune in to their natural world. Then regular observations may be rewarded on warm days by seeing the creatures emerge to feed or sun themselves. Log piles, heaps of grass cuttings, dead seed heads and fallen wood are all good places to keep an eye on, whether in wilder places or local parks, or in your own settings.

The patterns that frost makes on surfaces like glass or paving can be fine traceries to observe and record in photos and pictures. As they are an observable size, they will mean more to very young children than the idea that snowflakes have six points, or multiples thereof, but can only be seen under magnification.

Things to create

With little risk of setting fire to the surrounding vegetation, this is an ideal time to create a warming fire, as described in the last chapter. There are also a range of things to do with bare wood, peeling bark off and decorating hazel wands, or collecting elder to cut into short lengths and make into beads, as described in the activity below. Use willow to make winter stars, cracking the stem to create six sides and weaving them in and out to form a star. Try it, you will work it out.

With shorter days and bare trees, this is a lovely time to encourage the children to look at the colours of the sky and the tracery of branches. Practitioners can help children to recreate silhouette patterns on colourful backgrounds in a range of different ways, depending on the age and interests of the children.

 Activity: elder beads

Elder can be found everywhere, in towns and cities as well as the countryside, and it is a robust and vigorous shrub, so can be cut for the children's use. It has a structure similar to bamboo, with sections between joints that have a very soft centre that is easy to remove. Older children can use it to make whistles, but the easiest thing for young children is to make beads. They can help you to find the elder, and depending on their age and ability, can be helped to cut it with sharp secateurs (blunt ones will crush rather than cut, making the stem useless). There can be more cutting practice back at base as the stems are cut into short lengths. If they are short enough, the soft centres can be pushed out – the suitable tool to use will depend on the diameter of the wood. They can be threaded onto strings as they are, or peeled and coloured with paint or felt tip pens. See Figure 5.2 for a picture of elder and some beads.

Spring

Rapid and constant change makes Spring seem to last a long time in the UK, from the first snowdrops in late January to the froth of May blossom, but in fact the first signs overlap with winter and the last exuberances can be so warm as to feel like summer. These overlap times can be deceptive, causing enthusiastic gardeners to plant seeds too soon, or be caught by late May frosts. However, global warming does mean that we can start gardening earlier, particularly in towns and cities that are better insulated than exposed rural spots. Similarly, if you are going out and about, expect to see flowers in parks earlier than in the countryside, and expect to feel an edge to the wind in exposed places.

Figure 5.2   Elder and beads

Things to do

Now is the time to set vegetable seeds, according to the instructions on the packets or the advice of the donators. You could well end up with plenty of donations once parents are aware of your plans, as buying a packet of seeds is not as simple as it seems. Each one will usually contain far more than you are likely to need, unlike packets of flower seeds. This is particularly true of tomatoes, and once you have sent one home with every child you will still have an excess. If you are part of a cluster group of any kind, it is a good idea to coordinate your seed setting so that you have the care of one particular kind, and can then exchange with one another. Peas are good to grow as you can eat the new pods (mange tout), the immature pods (sugar snap) and the fully-grown peas. Being a legume, they also fix nitrogen in the soil, so are beneficial to your vegetable patch. Peas, beans, courgettes and tomatoes can be grown in every kind of container including hanging baskets, pots and bags, and most children will like most of them most of the time. Plants that climb will also tumble, down banks or out of baskets. Potatoes can be grown in pots or in stacks of old tyres – add a tyre to the stack and fill it with earth as the potatoes break through to increase your yield.

Salad crops like lettuce grow quickly, provided you water them, and children are much more likely to eat fresh food if they have grown and picked it themselves.

Things to eat

Celebrate the freshness of spring with the bounty of the hedgerow. Go for a walk and you will see the new leaves forming on hawthorn, another vigorous native shrub. This used to be called 'bread and cheese', which is a complete misnomer as in April, the time to harvest it, the taste is nutty. If you eat them straight from the bush pick the newest leaves from high enough up to avoid the risk of them having been watered by passing mammals. Do so sparingly to respect the plant, but it is a part of our connectivity with nature to gather its bounty. Plants then cease to become weeds and become instead our partners. This is a real adventure for your children.

A good case in point is the stinging nettle, which is a vegetable providing a good source of iron if picked before June (after that they are bitter and have a laxative effect). You will need gloves to gather new leaves and tips, to strip the leaves from the stems and to wash them, but as soon as they are cooked in no more than the water they were washed in, the sting disappears. Richard Mabey's books (listed in the Further reading section) are a good starting point to discovering the richness that is available to us, and spring and autumn are the best times to go foraging.

Another use for elder, used in winter for beads, is to create elderflower drinks. Collect a frothy white head per pint, and pick it over for bugs and dead growth, but do not wash them, or you will lose some of the flavour. Cut off as much stem as you can, put them in a jug and pour boiling water over them. Stir in some sugar, and leave to cool. Strain the liquid off and drink the taste of spring.

Things to observe

Children seem fascinated by the young of others – perhaps there is a certain kinship amongst them, and many settings will arrange outings to see, and sometimes to feed, lambs, etc. In the case study below, I describe how we brought young life into our nursery. These creatures can be handled, whereas nests spotted on walks should be observed and then left. If you have nest boxes in your outdoor areas, they will be chosen by birds who are accustomed to the noise and proximity of the children, so they can be observed more regularly.

 ## Case study: baby birds

In my nursery, we used to raise chicks and ducklings each year under a lamp in the dressing-up box, which underwent a change of use for a couple of weeks. I was assured that the young birds could withstand the attentions of 52 three- and four-year-olds, being made of cartilage rather than bone, and that certainly seemed true for the many years I undertook the task of raising them. The lamp was provided by the same farm that loaned the birds and their food. The ducklings were more fun, being cleverer, but they had a tendency to escape. The chicks were very obliging in that they put on the same amount of weight each day when weighed in a set of balances, the equivalent of one old-fashioned wooden clothes peg. After about a week, they would start to grow adult feathers and to smell, and so were returned to the farm that had loaned them to us. The children had the opportunity to observe and handle them, and to discuss their growth and their eventual destinations on our tables.

Things to create

As the plants and trees begin to sprout leaves and flowers, so too will animals begin to wake up or return. Children will often express their observations in their artwork, so providing the materials to do this is good practice, when it is done with imagination and creativity. In the next case study, I describe the process by which one child undertook such a piece of self-expression, one that might not have been served by the conventional collage materials on an art table. Some children's creativity takes other forms, and so their nest building might be just as likely to involve making a child-sized nest in the outdoor area, as a chocolate and shredded wheat one on the cooking table, or as a decorous tissue-paper creation on the art table.

 ## Case study: returning life

Our regular Forest School site was adjacent to some tall trees favoured by rooks, which began to return to the trees in early spring and to rebuild their nests. With no leaves on the trees we could see them clearly, and there was much discussion about which nests

(Continued)

(Continued)

would be chosen to be refurbished and why that might be. One boy was particularly interested, and on the second week after their return he set to out to replicate what he had seen on the ground. A long pole to denote the tree trunk was bare for two thirds of its length, then had sticks for branches sticking out at right-angles, quite accurately. At the top, he constructed a 'nest' of twigs and leaves and placed in it some round stones. He had taken at least half an hour over his creation, and when he had finished he looked at it with satisfaction. He then ignored it, and went off to play elsewhere. It had fulfilled its purpose in developing his understanding of what he had seen, and that was enough for him. I was excited enough to take its picture, but then I am an adult, and am concerned with product as well as process. That is my agenda, and it was not his.

Summer

Our UK summers are very variable, but whatever the weather is doing the sun will be at its strongest and so our children will need their sunscreen and our plants will need watering. But hopefully there will be plenty of opportunities to be out and about on adventurous outings while the days are long. July and August particularly should be times of plenty in the garden, offering easy opportunities for the children to try new healthy flavours.

Things to do

Involving the children in watering the pots and plants is another good way to help them to understand their world. If it is always the responsibility of adults, it will not engage them in any sense of ownership, and they will be less curious and less interested to try the produce. Putting that produce together to make picnics to eat outside will help, too – see the section below.

Now is an ideal time to venture further afield. Some settings find this difficult, but if you can take advantage of volunteer help from parents and students, you can see where you can get to by public transport, rather than using expensive coaches or minibuses. At the time of writing, the House of Commons is recommending that the DCSF looks at increasing the funding support for outings (2010: 12), so perhaps the situation in England will improve.

Your outing does not have to be to an exotic location, just different, and many children have few opportunities to use buses and trains when they are transported in the family car to most destinations, so using them makes the trip more of an adventure. And even a two-year-old can carry a rucksack with a bottle of water and a sandwich, particularly one they have made. When you arrive at your chosen spot, set up a base camp and allow the children some time to explore their new setting with you. Minute explorations of a new tree, patch of grass or daisy are fascinating for the very young, and as they grow older the chance to scramble over, under and behind trees and other obstacles is equally valuable.

If you have not grown your own riches, this is the time of year when local produce should be at its most prolific. Taking the children to your local shop, market or farm to pick their own will be an adventure to encourage a healthy diet. The children can then be involved in their preparation.

Things to eat

Washing lettuce and strawberries, and slicing tomatoes and cucumbers can tempt even the most reluctant. There are tasks that can be performed by all ages and stages. Making picnics to eat in the setting or on outings is limited only by the imagination of the practitioners. Baby courgettes can be stuffed with cream cheese, for example, while cherry tomatoes in yellow, orange and red are designed to be popped into the mouth instead of sweeties. Allow the children to try their own combinations of sandwich fillings, even if they are unusual. Marmite and strawberries might not work for you, but you may have the next Heston Blumenthal in your group.

Things to observe

In Chapter 2, we considered some of the effects of the sun, to dry out water paintings and other materials, and summer is usually a good time to observe these effects. Plants that are not watered will quickly wilt, and as quickly recover when given the water. Our skins change colour in the sun, prompting discussions on skin care.

Getting out and about offers opportunities to observe other places such as the beach. If there are rock pools, these can provide windows into other worlds. If not, then collecting stones and shells offers opportunities for sorting and matching.

Things to create

On hot days, the best thing to create is shade, and this can be combined with creating children's own spaces. Children love making dens, whether in settings or out in the woods. The simplest versions can be made by draping a cloth over a table, or by tying a tarpaulin between two branches. More sophisticated dens may look closer in design to a tent or a bender, but on hot days be sure to encourage a through breeze, as they can become very stuffy and make the inhabitants feel unwell.

In the wood, find a long branch to lean on a tree, then shorter branches to lean on that to make a lean-to shelter. Once you have a frame, you can add grasses or bracken to insulate, and your shelter will be cool and shady, not hot and stuffy. Taking a tarpaulin with you widens the designs you can create, and offers a waterproof base to pile rucksacks on. The following activity describes how I created a basic tipi from a cheap tarpaulin, something which while less than perfect, I have found useful in my Forest School sessions. You may be able to improve on my design.

 Activity: making a tipi

Using a very elderly sewing machine and a cheap tarpaulin from a warehouse of outdoor goods, I cut out triangles from one side of the rectangle and inserted them into the other side to create a shape that could be wrapped around a cone of sticks. I attached ties to the top (short) side, and peg loops to the bottom (long) side. Figure 5.3 shows the end result, which many of you will be able to improve on, but it has worked for groups with me. Once you have constructed your own cover, you can involve the children. You will need six poles of similar lengths – which will depend on the size of the tarpaulin, but are likely to be between two and three metres in length, and a piece of rope to tie around the top. When I am running Forest School sessions, I hide them near the base camp between sessions. The children and I agreed that they would need to carry one pole between two, not because they are heavy but because they are likely to swing around and clonk others when carried by one child. Balance three in a tripod and tie once – the tying has to be done by an adult because of the height. Then place the other three in between them, and tie securely. Wrap the cover around the poles, tie it and peg it down. In my experience, once three- and four-year-olds have been shown how to do this twice, they will take over getting it set up, apart from tying the top.

Autumn

As with spring, this season can seem long and varied. It starts with what is often an Indian summer in September, and ends in the damp darkness of November. Nature is busy wrapping up and shutting down to protect

Figure 5.3 My eccentric tipi

itself from the cold, but that process offers some wonderful opportunities for adventures.

Things to do

Untidy places are the kindest for wildlife, so taking the risk of leaving a part of your outdoor area with dead and decaying plant material in it is a positive step, and will give the children many more creatures to look at. Some creatures will need to find places to stay safely over winter, but if you struggle to achieve that unkempt corner, here is another idea. You can combine providing hibernation spots with creating a structure that will look interesting and purposeful and will help an endangered species. Stag beetles are in decline, and one way to help them is to create a stag beetle pyramid for them to lay their eggs in, and for their larva to live in (which can be for up to seven years). It is easy to do, and also provides hibernation sites for other small creatures like ladybirds and lacewings. Dig a hole 50–75 centimetres deep and the same across. Stack into it a range of logs and branches of different sizes, making sure that you use untreated timber. You can do this to whatever design the children choose, as the beetles are not fussy. Pack the earth back in around the logs to hold them in place. Leave it to degrade. As the wood breaks down, the creatures move in.

As you walk to your wilder spaces, remember how you felt about fallen leaves when you were a child. They are there to be kicked and jumped in and thrown. In the next chapter, there is the ultimate example of this, so here I will focus on the drifts of naturally occurring leaves. Jump in leaves.

Figure 5.4 A five-year-old stag beetle pyramid

Not to do so is to deprive your children of natural fun. If you choose the leaves that are lying deep in parks and in wilder places and the children have the right footwear, and you can wash/wipe their hands before eating, then the risks are minimal. On streets you may need to be more cautious, because of animal litter and road dangers, but learning about that difference is a part of learning to keep yourself safe for the children. If you cannot access a wild leaf collection, I suggest collecting a sackful and taking them into the setting for the children to play with. Once they have been kicked and thrown then the best of them can be used for creative activities.

Things to eat

Autumn is the time for berries in our wilder spaces. I am horrified by the number of students that I work with who will not pick blackberries in the wild, which to me is the ultimate symbol of the nature-deficit disorder (Louv, 2010) at the heart of our society. Please do not let your children grow up with that attitude. Mabey (2007: 112) describes how blackberry seeds have been found in the stomach of Neolithic Essex man: this is the ultimate natural food. Encourage your children to identify the ripe fruit and to eat them. Other berries are less user-friendly, and children under three years of age are best encouraged to leave all other berries in the wild alone, but the risks are minimal. The only berries of serious harm in the UK are the yew and ivy berries. The UK government Food Standards Agency has ideas for wild harvesting at www.eatwell.gov.uk/healthydiet/seasonsandcelebrations/hedgerowharvest but a good basic rule is to stick to blackberries if you are unsure. Of the other most common fruit you will find, elderberries look very tempting and are a wonderful source of vitamin C when cooked, but contains toxins if eaten raw. Hawthorn berries make a beautiful jelly, but eaten raw are mostly stone and an acquired taste. Wild apples of all colours are too sour to eat, but also make lovely jellies of all different colours.

Pumpkins ripen in the autumn, and are cheap to buy. Settings often buy one to cut a face into, and discard the flesh which has been such hard work to dig out. Made into soup it will connect the children with the fruit in a more complete way, as you tell them the stories connected to it. I include apples (from my garden) in my pumpkin soup recipe, to add interest.

As you collect and use the bounty of nature from the wild and from the garden, also collect the seeds to sow in the spring. Ask the children to draw pictures of the plant to put on the paper bags you store them in. The storing and then growing, and the drawing of the plant, helps them to understand the cycles of life in a deeper and more meaningful way.

Things to observe

Point out to children the swallows and swifts lining up on the overhead wires for their departure on migration. A wonderful outing would be to one of the hot-spots of inward migration, usually geese. Contact your local wildlife trust for ideas.

This is a good time of year for spotting fungi. In countries where the collection of these for the table is more common there are ways to get your basket checked for rogue elements, but we do not have that facility, so I generally have a rule of looking but not touching. It is a shame, as there are many tasty dishes in the wild, but I do not feel confident in identifying many of them, so this is where I acknowledge my limitations. Perhaps if we can support a new generation to become in tune with their environment there will be more of them who can see fungi as a food source and not just a wonder to watch.

Generally, nature is preparing for winter, and expeditions to spot the signs can be fun, or watching around your own setting can also be profitable. Are the squirrels hiding nuts? Are the toads, frogs and hedgehogs looking for hibernation sites? Are the days getting shorter?

Things to create

Creating hibernation homes can be an outdoor activity. Hedgehogs are a declining species, and the British Hedgehog Preservation Society has some simple designs on its website www.britishhedghogs.org for 'hibernacula' that the children can make. Leaf collections can be used to create collage pictures as they are, or you can laminate the children's favourite ones for sorting and pattern making. The shape of leaves often echoes the outline shape of the tree, and older children can be encouraged to spot where this similarity exists, which may shape their collage designs.

 Points for practice

The points of risk and opportunities for adventure in this chapter have for the most part been implicit, and around the ability of the practitioners to tune in to the natural world. In Chapter 3 I indicated how important training is to help staff to feel at ease in the natural world, and I reiterate that here. However, a good set of books for identification will back this up, as no one should be expected to remember all the details of our flora and fauna all of the time. It also helps the children's understanding of the importance of literacy if they see that adults use books and the internet for reference and to confirm their understanding. Field guides should be small enough to be carried on expeditions, so you will need a range of big books for indoors, and small ones for outdoors. Do not buy these all at once, but aim to build them up over time as the understanding of the practitioners in your settings changes and develops, but do budget for book purchases to support all areas of learning outside the classroom.

Discussion points

Trawl your memories, and those of friends:

- What are your best memories from each of the four seasons?
- What did you learn and understand as a result of these?
- Could these become activities for your children?

Further reading

Ellaway, A., Kirk, A., Macintyre, S. and Mutrie, N. (2007) 'Nowhere to play? The relationship between the location of outdoor play areas and deprivation in Glasgow', *Health and Place*, 13(2): 557–61.

Mabey, R. (2009) *Wild Cooking*. London: Vintage.

Mabey, R. (2007) *Food For Free*. London: Collins.

Ward, J. (2008) *I Love Dirt*. Boston, USA: Shambhala Publications, Inc.

Wilson, R. (2008) *Nature and Young Children*. Abingdon: David Fulton.

Heuristic Play

> ## Chapter objectives
>
> In this chapter, I aim to:
>
> - link heuristic play to outdoor play
> - discuss the implications of heuristic learning for all ages and stages of children
> - link heuristic play with holistic learning.

Introduction

Heuristic play is an expression familiar to early years practitioners in the UK and elsewhere. Goldschmied and Jackson (2004) described the application of the idea of heuristic learning to our youngest children, and it was they who coined the term heuristic play, to describe the investigation of objects and their functions by babies and toddlers. The origins of heuristic play thus lie in the concept of heuristic education, where the learner is trained to find things out for themselves, which in other words is discovery learning (from the Greek 'heuriskein', which means to discover), another familiar term. As an approach to learning, it can be linked to 'trial-and-error' learning, or to using existing knowledge to develop a 'rule-of-thumb' to apply to problem solving. In some applications, the training of the learner involves the teacher in asking provocative questions designed to stimulate curiosity, which connects it back in history to the Socratic teaching method of question and exploratory debate. It has more usually been written about as it is applied to teaching older pupils, as described by Morsanyi (2009) and Burke (2005), often associated with business management and computer science. This explains why Goldschmied's work was so innovative, in that she took this familiar idea and adapted it for younger children in what was then an unfamiliar way.

Working with younger children in outdoor environments gives us the advantage of utilising their natural curiosity about the world and how it works, thus obviating the need for some of the questioning, but not all. Their instinct towards building a model of the world through empirical, exploratory learning (as described by Piaget) means that a heuristic approach feels both appropriate and in harmony with the children's natural processes in outdoor learning. It also means that the learning will be holistic, as the environment envelops the children's experiences. Outdoor experiences offer the opportunity of heuristic learning to all pre-school children, not just the youngest ones. 'Trial and error' will inevitably lead to some levels of risk, as children push the boundaries to discover where they lie. It is part of the learning process, and it is the sensitivity of the practitioner that enables the child to take such risks in a 'safe enough' environment.

In this chapter, I wish to explore the relationship between the work of Goldschmied and Jackson and the outdoor agenda, and to link it to quality learning experiences for older pre-school children. It is the first of two themes, the second being creativity which I shall tackle in the next chapter, both of which explore the opportunities for holistic learning in outdoor experiences. When we consider the learning that takes place through the investigations of the learner, we will need to consider the relational balance between the practitioner as facilitator, as partner and as observer, rather than as the practitioner in a traditional teaching role. In each section, I will consider each of these roles in turn.

A part of the role of facilitator is in the management of risk. The discussion will engage with the risks inherent in allowing access for free exploration of natural objects to very young children, and why I believe that such risks are legitimate. It will consider what adventures are for the very young, and how the concept of adventure broadens and deepens with age and experience. Practitioners' perceptions are also based on age and experience, and the interplay between the two can enable or disable the children's investigations, as can be seen in the case study which follows. The role of the adult as observer will also be a part of risk management, as well as a chance to record the children's interests and achievements.

The practitioner as partner offers opportunities to support open-ended exploration as outlined by Goldschmied and Jackson (2004) but also to question as in the tradition of heuristic learning described above, which may be a chance to find out together (perhaps by trial and error) about some aspect of the outdoor environment. It may also be a chance to extend play and learning by offering additional resources or by helping with tool use.

Case study: flying dragons

My first encounter with children climbing trees caused me to review my own perceptions of risk. I had been an enthusiastic tree-climber as a child, but as an adult taking other people's children into the woods I was less confident about allowing them to climb. Fortunately, I was with a more experienced practitioner with my first class of four-year-olds in a wood with a wealth of large fallen trees. One in particular caught the children's attention, as the thick fallen branches reached out two metres above the ground, and would bounce in a satisfying way. Once the group were settled, and the play was under way, we split into natural groupings according to the competence and confidence of the adults and the children. I worked with a less able group, helping them to explore how to walk along a log on the ground. My colleague was engaged with a more able group. Up the branches she went, up went the more confident children, and soon there was a row of them astride the branch, which had become a dragon to ride in the wind. What an exciting adventure they had! Yes, there were risks – they could have fallen, and fallen onto other branches. The branch they were on could have broken under the weight. I had to trust that the leader knew her tree, and that the children who had followed were competent enough climbers. She was the leader, and the responsibility was with her, an issue we will return to in Chapter 8, but it did make me reflect on how I could enable such an exciting adventure to occur when I was in charge. It reinforced the importance of knowing your children, knowing your space and using your own competencies and those of the others in your team to best advantage.

Under twos

Treasure baskets to facilitate heuristic play are now almost commonplace in settings for babies and toddlers. As soon as they can be propped in a sitting position, they can have a basket of objects to explore, mouthing, banging and rolling to find out the true nature of each object, and what it can do. The objects in the basket are everyday, commonplace and made of natural materials. Moving this familiar play into less familiar outdoor spaces not only adds a new dimension but also gives us the opportunity to re-engage with the theory and practice of heuristic play, as we evaluate what is needed in an outdoor approach to heuristic play in order to keep the essential elements as defined by its originators.

At this youngest age or stage, the key question for the child is 'What are these objects like?', as they explore the treasures presented to them. They are traditionally placed in a basket to limit the number and classification of objects to something both manageable and attractive.

The key question for the practitioner is how to widen the children's horizons to enable them to find out about as many objects as are relevant to them, in a measured and controlled way. The everyday, the common place and those made from natural materials are grouped according to a classification decided by the practitioner. Are they kitchen objects, or a collection of objects from another area of their environment?

As facilitators, we are providing objects to explore that provide keys to their environments, and doing this outside offers a new range of classifications, whether on a beach or in the garden or in the wood. This adds to the exploratory treasure basket the link to where the children are situated at that time, locating the experience in its context. Taking an empty 'basket' (or other portable receptacle) with you when you go on outings, to collect everyday objects for the babies to explore, is a way to link them to their environment. Arranging them to look attractive in the container will add interest and harmony, which is an important step in the process. Toddlers can become partners, and help with the collection and arrangement themselves. It is a way of bringing the environment to the baby, to provide them with space and time to explore and engage with what is around them.

The risks we are dealing with are firstly those of hygiene – are the objects clean enough? This may require some ingenuity to find sources of water for washing, or utilisation of wipes on the parts that will be mouthed. If it is really not possible, you may have to bring them back to the setting for exploration – I have soaked seashells in the cleaning formula used for sterilising feeding bottles to enable a child with a weak immune system to have access to them. But do use common sense about allowing children the opportunity to access some less-than-perfectly clean stones, cones and shells, or their immune systems will never develop.

Other risks around small parts being eaten or stuffed up the nose, and large objects being dropped on toes, are mitigated by the close observation and non-intrusive supervision of the practitioner. Recordings of Elinor Goldschmied working with babies before her death in 2009 show that she did facilitate reasonable risks, her precautionary measures centring on the role of the practitioner as observer. She had a common-sense approach, as many experienced practitioners have. My mother tells me that she knew I would be artistic because as a baby I stuffed daisies up my nose, whereas my sister ate worms. She became a nurse. We both have robust immune systems.

The role of observer cannot be underestimated in this way of working. It is the observations that, apart from keeping the baby safe, will allow the adult to mediate between the environment and the child. Noting what they are interested in, following this up in subsequent baskets, adding and subtracting objects, will enable the child's developing map of their world to expand and flourish. While their eyesight is still developing, this map depends on caring practitioners providing real concrete

Figure 6.1   A garden basket

materials that enable them to use all their senses to add to their growing understanding. The garden, the woods and the beach can all be reached in this way, laying the foundations of understanding and familiarity to build on as they grow. The example in Figure 6.1 contains objects found in gardens, and the greatest risk shown is from the flaking (man-made) paint on one of the handles.

Twos and threes

As children become more mobile and communicative, their interest in the objects around them develops from 'what it is' to 'what it can become'. Their exploration is still open-ended, as they explore systems of representation (Ashton et al., 2009: 10) and symbolic representation. Their learning is built on their previous explorations of objects, emphasising how important the continuity of the learning journey is (DfES, 2007: 3.2). Babies who have experienced the richness of the outdoor environment described above will move more quickly to explore wider opportunities in the next phase of their development.

The holistic sensory environment of outdoor settings offers a rich palette for flexible and fluid thinking. Being mobile allows them to combine objects in unique ways and explore new possibilities. One important new experience will be to walk, crawl and roll on a variety of surfaces. Colleagues involved with outdoor play with this age group in urban areas are reporting that children are coming to them with no experience of walking on uneven surfaces, for example rough grass or rutted paths. This means that they have no experience of how to keep their own balance. They become fearful when presented with surfaces that are not man-made. This represents an alarming gap in the kinaesthetic learning of toddlers that needs to be addressed.

We should not underestimate the creative abilities of our youngest children. For example, almost all children at this age enjoy simulating sharing 'cups of tea', or whatever their cultural norm of social sharing is. In indoor settings, there may well be child-sized versions of the equipment necessary, but in the wild there may not be anything that looks to the adult eye anything like a cup. As can be seen in the case study below, a child accustomed to being outside can conjure teacups from very unpromising material. Exercising the imagination in this way is to open up possibilities of creative links that are important in later formal learning.

 Case study: teatime with pirates

I was out with a group of two-year-olds on a well-established Forest School session. The base camp included a raft of logs with others piled on it, which had become a pirate ship. A few children were engaged with one of the adults in constructing a mast for the ship, and one child decided to supply us all with tea while they worked. Perhaps she had observed this behaviour in adults when workmen were busy in her home. She searched the edge of the wood for plantain leaves, which became saucers, and collected rounded stones which she placed on the leaves. These were our cups, and everyone happily 'drank' from them. Not only did she use her imagination to provide the tea, but we all used ours to collude with her creations. No adults challenged her creativity with exhortations about dirty stones or unknown leaves, and we were all 'safe enough'.

As they become more sociable in their play, the representational aspects of found objects may be mediated through social interactions, as can be seen in the case study. Lucas and Claxton (2010: 14) highlight how important this is in widening our learning potential through social interactions. In this example, the child had expanded her understanding of the potential of a stone, perhaps by searching for a link between a cup and anything in her surroundings and finding the shared property of roundness. She had then enabled the rest of the group to perceive this shared property, without having to go through the same process that she had been through. This is a demonstration of how social learning can, in some cases, be more efficient than solitary learning, a point I return to below.

At this age, there are opportunities for the child to investigate the objects in their environment alone, in partnership with other children or in partnership with an adult. What they gain in understanding may be useful in every one of these examples, so it is important that the practitioner as facilitator enables all of these to occur. As an adult partner, they may be able to use superior height or strength or reach – in the case study, the adult working on the construction of the mast was able to use these attributes to force a long branch between the logs on the raft. She was, however, working in partnership with the children and following their directions as often as offering her own, and none of them had complete mastery of the task; the mast still fell over several times before they had wedged and tied it securely. Being a partner in play successfully is often about finding your own inner child, without becoming childish.

What is being observed by the practitioner is becoming increasingly complex, as is inevitable when holistic heuristic opportunities are enabled. Qualities are being discovered, skills are being developed and minds are expanding as a multiplicity of neural pathways are created or reinforced. Being in woods, gardens, parks or on the beach offers opportunities limited only by the practitioner's imagination and bravery. The following activity gives an example of an activity that can be adapted for all outdoor settings and is not high-risk. Another example of adult imagination can be seen in Figure 6.2, where leaves are deliberately corralled for the express purpose of creating a place where they can be jumped in and thrown about.

Figure 6.2   The leaf pit at Roehampton University

Activity: puddle stew

Mud seems to be very popular at this age, so the opportunity to combine it with imaginative play makes this activity a winner. Having taken water out into the wood with you to drink or to douse fire, you can spare some to help a child make puddle stew. You will need to provide a trowel or hand fork for the child to hollow out a bowl in the earth, and a sturdy stick or spoon for stirring. They can collect a mix of ingredients, for example small pieces of bark, seeds and leaves, and pile them ready to make the stew. They may also like to find some larger leaves as plates to dish up the stew on to. Help them to pour some water into their bowl, and stir to mix in some of the earth. Add the ingredients, and keep stirring until the water and ingredients are satisfyingly muddy. Add more water if required. When all the fun of stirring has been extracted, they can serve up the stew on the plates for an equally satisfying pretend meal – a simple but effective idea.

Fours and fives

Heuristic holistic investigations become increasingly complex as children build on their prior experiences and use them in their growing social experiences. One manifestation of this can be described as being 'extended narratives'. Tim Waller (2007) describes this phenomena in his paper listed below, and I have also experienced it (see the case study below). It would appear that at this age when literacy is still largely oral, narratives serve complex social and cognitive functions. It would also seem to be a phenomenon of the outdoors, as there are few records of it occurring over time indoors. I can only think of the Tidy House (Steedman, 1983), where the narrative is between older (eight-year-old) children and is a recorded activity for a writing task. Perhaps there is a link back to our pre-literate selves when the passing on of narratives such as Beowulf created social and cultural cohesion. Whatever its function, there is a need for a sensitive adult observer to record, and to add resources if necessary to facilitate this important social construction of complex ideas.

Lucas and Claxton (2010: 115) talk about socialised learning and collective intelligence as ways to advance children's thinking. We are used to researchers grouping together to unpick problems, so why should we be surprised when children do the same, to develop their understanding of the way the world works. Rather, it is a skill we should be encouraging and developing, as it will be so useful in future worlds of the workplace to create communities of learning. It is a skill-set ideally suited to wilder outdoor activities, as children solve problems of fire lighting, making shelters and transporting themselves and their gear from place to place.

The practitioner as partner is important at this age, to take advantage of their growing independence and competence, and before more formal schooling begins in England. Expeditions that are longer and more adventurous can be planned, as children who have had the experiences described in previous sections will be able to be active partners in planning and carrying out such events. In the UK, the major outdoor organisations all have an interest in getting younger children outside, and will collude to provide suitable destinations within reach of settings.

 ## Case study: the chocolate factory

In a nearby school I had been working with the early years class, supporting their Forest School sessions in 2004, and had then left the teacher to carry on. When I returned for a visit in 2005, she drew my attention to a group of children around a tree. They had slid long poles through the lower branches to create levers, and there were logs and branches arranged around the base in a way that showed they had significance for the game. The teacher explained that it was based on the recent Johnny Depp film of Charlie and the Chocolate Factory. It was a complicated, child-led game, the adults being occasionally invited to taste different flavours, but otherwise we were not needed. The numbers and gender mix of children ebbed and flowed throughout the session, as often seems to happen with a well-established game. My colleague informed me that it had been going on for a number of weeks. When I returned again, in 2008, the game was still going on! It had changed, as had the children, but somehow the children had passed the idea on from class to class. The only continuity we could identify in one instance between one year group and the next was that a sibling had been part of the original group and two years later the younger brother had come to the school and had carried on with the idea. The link with the original film had faded, only the production of chocolate with a variety of flavours persisted, with the levers still to the fore. Still, there was a mix of children of different gender spending a part of their Forest School time each week in the factory.

During my visits in that season, I witnessed the introduction of a magic key to the game, and a move towards a different story base, around the defence of the key and the development of its powers to turn objects into gold, so perhaps another shared experience was becoming more dominant. But the levers and the use of other logs and branches continued. I often reflect on that four-year-long story game, and speculate endlessly about its function. Hopefully one day it will be the subject of further research.

Over fives

The formal curriculum in England clicks in for children on their fifth birthday. In other countries it is later, but as children grow towards their seventh birthday most will have activities on offer that the adults at least acknowledge are linked to identifiable formal learning targets. This does not mean that they have to be indoors, or that the heuristic holistic element is any less important. Appreciating the sensory qualities of objects and exploring their potential is still a part of any valuable lesson, and being outside enables all learning styles to be fully engaged. To illustrate my point, I will consider four activity options available to practitioners without specialised training or knowledge, just an interest in learning outside the classroom, and how they link into subject areas in the formal curriculum.

 ## Activity: discovering collections on the beach

Many children will naturally start collecting stones, shells and minerals such as pieces of quartz when they are on the beach. You can pick up on their natural interests, or stimulate them with examples of your own. Shells will tend to accumulate on the tide line, and pieces of quartz or fossils at the base of cliffs. Stones may be scattered across the whole beach area. Children will establish their own initial collection criteria – perhaps by colour, size or shape. When they have amassed a range of examples, they may re-sort their collection into subsets. This is mathematical thinking, creating sets by sorting. Shells are the discarded homes of crustaceans, bringing in opportunities for biological, geographical and environmental learning. On their return to settings, they can be used creatively in collage or in decorations. Stones and minerals are rubbed smooth by the action of the water, leading to scientific

(Continued)

(Continued)

> discussions about friction. They may indicate the ages of the cliffs, leading to historical and geological research. On return to the settings they can be polished or used to create tessarea and mosaic. Reference books on shells, fossils and rocks will be a useful resource.

In the activities above the role of the practitioner is an important and sensitive one. Observing when a child's interests can be picked up on, and facilitating its development, requires openness and flexibility. These qualities often come from leaders who are comfortable with their surroundings and their role, emphasising the importance of preparation

Figure 6.3   Pheasant tracks

 Activity: experimenting with tracks and signs

When walking in wilder areas or indeed observing any muddy patch, children will be able to see the tracks left by the animals and birds that share their environment, but that they might otherwise

be unaware of. Figure 6.3 shows pheasant tracks which are large, clear and frequent in rural areas. Small, clear and frequent are the dainty pairs of dots of deer tracks. In urban areas, the bird prints may be smaller, and the animal prints, such as dogs and cats, larger. It is fun to collect these – they can be recorded (depending on the solidity of the mud) by rubbings, taking plaster casts, drawings and photographs. Children may also look out for other signs of animals passing, such as hairs caught on twigs and fences. These can then be researched back in the settings, and children can work out their possible routes of travel and possible reasons for those routes. A game between two teams can then take place, where one side lays a track for the others to follow. I played this as a Girl Guide, leaving arrows of twigs on the ground and coloured cottons on twigs. Children can agree their own signals for each other, and the followers need to wait ten minutes for the trailblazers to start. When they catch them up, the roles are reversed. If they fail to catch them, the conventional sign for 'gone home' is a ring of stones with one in the middle. This game addresses the targets for the personal, social and emotional (PSE) curriculum, as well as linking to geography, biology and history (in the stories of tracking by hunters).

Figure 6.4 A home-made woodland creature

for outings and expeditions with pre-visits and risk assessments. We should be happy to acknowledge that there will inevitably be things that each of us do not know about the aspect of the environment that the child is interested in, and so we can become their learning partner as well as the person leading the group. This is a positive message to send to the child, that none of us can know everything, but that all of us can be open to new learning. The practitioner will need to be alert to the potential of the situation, both positive and negative, so that the child stays safe enough, the environment is safe enough, and the learning is good enough.

 ## Activity: exploring homes and habitats

I have already mentioned opportunities for spotting birds' nests, in Chapter 5, but where children are being helped to 'tune in' to tracks, they may well also begin to spot holes and indentations in undergrowth that indicate that animals may have rested or slept there. It is very difficult for novices, adult or child, to accurately work out which animals were there, and that really is not important initially. Launching the idea that such places exist and are important is quite sufficient. One way to do this is to encourage the children to make their own wild creature out of grass and twigs, and then to build a home for them. This can prompt extension activities around what such animals might eat, and their care needs. Figure 6.4 is one such animal, made by a five-year-old by tying grass into a knot and sticking legs, wings and eyes into the bundle. Once again, the activity links to PSE, biology, geography and history, and can work very well with projects about houses back in the classroom.

 ## Activity: sounds of the environment

Whilst children in this age group may have fully developed hearing, their capacity to judge the direction of sounds will still be developing, as this is based on experience. There is also a rise in the number of hearing difficulties being diagnosed in children, so activities about listening and hearing will help children to sharpen their awareness and hone their hearing skills. It also improves concentration and attention skills. Listening games encourage children to identify the sounds around them and expands their knowledge of what to listen for, whether it is bird song, traffic or animal noises. These games can be as simple as sitting quietly for a minute and then listing all the heard sounds. Do not worry if you cannot identify different bird songs at this stage. An interest in such things will encourage children to expand their knowledge as they grow older. Progressing to the sounds we make when we move through the environment will help children to expand their vocabularies to include the words we use to describe the sounds, for example crackling, snapping and crunching. Chants and songs can turn these into instant shared creativity as you walk along, or as you recapture your adventures at times of reflection. Back in the classroom, these words can be used to make poetry and stories. Children can become very innovative when making music in wilder areas. Practitioners with skills in working elder can help them to create panpipes and various kinds of whistle. Those of us less confident with elder can help children to find percussive instruments such as logs to drum and wooden beaters to bang together. One group I worked with found that a stand of sycamore seedlings made a different clackerty sound when brushed with twigs. Some plant knowledge is useful here – sycamore self-seeds so easily that to use these plants in this way was not an environmental issue. I have found that music making can evolve in different ways in wilder places. It has arisen from one child's discovery of a sound and been built into a music-making session at that moment, or instruments have been created to be used later. Creating musical accompaniment to songs around the campfire adds another dimension to the sharing nature of this event. These activities link to the science of sounds, the creativity of music and to acts of communication. The biology of hearing can come in, too, particularly when comparing the hearing of the wildlife to our own abilities.

〜〜 Points for practice

Being ready to take advantage of opportunities as they occur means being both flexible and prepared. When going on expeditions this inevitably means carrying equipment with you. What you carry will vary according to the age and stage of your children and your destination. Wilder working at some distance from settings is more usual for children over the age of two, but all ages like to go to the beach. We are fortunate in the UK that most beach locations enable us to get wheeled transport reasonably adjacent to a beach, making the transportation of items easier.

Wilder working usually involves carrying more items for further distances, unless you are going for a simple nature ramble. I try to

(Continued)

(Continued)

get most of my Forest School kit into one rucksack, and when I meet a new group our first session will include them unpacking my rucksack and working out why everything is there. The following list contains some ideas that a Level 3 Forest School practitioner might carry in his/her rucksack for use with a group, to include opportunities for fire lighting and cooking:

Boundary tape/markers
Hand wipes/gel
First aid kit, including a foil blanket
Appropriate storage – rucksack/box
Tarpaulin
Secateurs
Loppers/folding pruning saw
Knives and/or potato peelers
Ropes and string
Children's work gloves
Fire lighting kit
Digital camera

In addition, s/he might need to carry the following items separately:

Water carriers
Fire container (if no suitable pit available)
Grill
Kettle and cups
Popcorn popper
Cooking pot and utensils

Other items may be useful, such as magnifiers and collecting boxes, but everything has to be carried in and out, so it is better to rely on the bounty of nature where possible. Individual children often carry their own additional clothing and water bottle, which helps. But these lists give practitioners some idea of the level of commitment needed for successful wild working.

 ## Discussion points

Consider the equipment lists above and discuss them with your team:

- What would you include and why?
- What would you exclude and why?
- Is there anything particularly important that you feel has been left out?
- What case would you make for including it, including curriculum links?

Further reading 📖

Hughes, A. (2010) *Developing Play for the Under Threes: The Treasure Basket and Heuristic Play*. Abingdon: Routledge.

Tucker, P. and Irwin, J. (2009) 'Physical activity behaviors during the preschool years', *Child Health and Education*, 1(3): 134–45.

Waller, T. (2007) 'The Trampoline Tree and the Swamp Monster with 18 heads': outdoor play in the Foundation Stage and Foundation Phase', *Education 3–13*, 35(4): 393–407.

White, J. (2008) *Playing and Learning Outdoors*. London: Routledge.

Natural Creativity

Chapter objectives

In this chapter, I aim to:

- link creativity to outdoor play
- discuss the implications of creativity for all ages and stages of children
- link creativity to lifelong learning
- think about the professional impact of enabling creativity.

Introduction

Whilst natural creativity has been touched on in most chapters, in this chapter I intend to focus exclusively on natural creativity, beginning with a discussion of the importance of all creativity to the intellectual development of children and to the future of society. The year 2009 was the European Year of Creativity and Innovation, a sign of the importance placed on creativity in European society. In 2007, the Lisbon Conference to prepare for the event made some interesting points about the importance of creativity to children, adults and society. The conference presentations linked creativity to social inclusion, pointing out that creativity is not a separate faculty that some people have and others do not, but is a function of human intelligence (Wimmer, 2007). When discussing school development, the statement was made that 'Creativity is a balance between freedom, authority, skill and speculation. It can be taught, but you have to loosen up the system to let it happen. You can't have creative learning without creative teaching' (Wimmer, 2007). When discussing the importance of creativity to society, the thoughts of the conference echoed those of Sir John Harvey-Jones, that creativity is essential for the future of successful industry and business (Robinson,

2001: 193). It is a key to innovation and to the kind of lateral thinking that prompts the kind of discoveries, changes and developments that are essential to stop society stagnating and declining. This places it at the root of all good education.

Traditionally it has been easier to facilitate the different forms of children's creativity in early years settings than it has been with school-aged children, as the younger ones have not been so constricted by the demands of a formal curriculum. It has been suggested that not only is creativity fundamental to advances in all areas of everyday life (Alexander, 2009b: 51), but that it is the crowded formal English curriculum that squeezes it out of children and teachers at the present (Alexander, 2009a: 18). It is easier to enable creativity to take place in an environment where children have the freedom to be innovative, flexible and adaptable, for example in good quality early years settings. Outdoor spaces are also predisposed to be used in this way, provided that the adults sharing those spaces are equally innovative, flexible and adaptable. Being outside offers the opportunity to provide an environment which stimulates aesthetic sensitivity, emotional development, lateral thinking and intuition, and which continues the natural creativity which exists in all children from their earliest stages of development. Self-expression facilitated outdoors has fewer boundaries, physical, psychological or emotional, than indoors and therefore can have a greater power.

I hope that I am making it clear that I believe that creative activities are extremely important for the healthy development of children and societies. The adventures and risks associated with such activities will be psychological and emotional, and may be physical. By that, I mean that to explore and express oneself involves each of us in engaging with our own self-awareness and self-expression, and opening these up to external scrutiny, which will inevitably expose our vulnerabilities. Fortunately, not only are most children comfortable with this process but also most early years practitioners are by training and inclination protective and caring toward the children in their settings. The emotional adventures can therefore be fully explored, as the risks are reasonable, provided that they are sensitively handled. The physical adventures and risks around tool use and the exploration of environments will need to be assessed as the opportunities occur.

Creativity is not restricted to subjects normally described as the arts, but occurs in all subjects when the participants find innovative and original solutions to problems, make connections and see new relationships. For example, in the following case study, I describe an example of mathematical creativity. However, in this chapter, I will suggest ideas for creative activities that do fall into subject headings recognisable as artistic. This should not be a concern to practitioners who do not consider themselves to be artistic, as facilitating creativity is about being innovative, flexible and adaptable, and children do not judge our artistic merit any more than we should judge their output by those criteria.

Artistic creativity can enable children to express feelings that are too big to be encompassed by conventional forms of communication, feelings that the environment can engender in all of us. Whether it is something big like the glory of a morning, or something small like the discovery of a tiny bug, the feelings are so big as to be difficult to express, particularly for children whose vocabulary is still restricted by their experiences. Having another medium to support that expression can enable them to develop their understanding and to assimilate the feelings into their developing cognition. The added element of being outdoors can provide opportunities for multi-channel communication, expression and development, and it can be bigger, louder and more elemental. Eaude (2008) describes this process as one of developing a personal narrative, helping us to understand who we are and what our place in the world is.

 Case study: mathematical creativity

Arriving in a familiar wood for a Forest School session with a well-established group of three- and four-year-olds, we found that tree surgeons had felled a couple of trees, logged the main trunks and chipped the smaller growth. We had a pile of logs between one and three metres long, and a pile of golden wood chips to dispose of. The children decided that they would like to line the path around the outside of the wood with the logs (not the path to their base camp, as they preferred to keep that secret) and fill the space in between the logs with the chips. Great ingenuity and teamwork were involved in finding ways to roll, pull and push the logs into position, and to find receptacles to carry the chips. The most original problem solving went on, however, when three boys found that there was a gap in the line of logs, and they needed to measure which log would fit into the gap. After some debate, one of them lay down in the gap and they decided how much of his length fitted the space. They then went over to the logs and measured him against the logs to find the best fit. It was a fine example of creative practical mathematics.

Storytelling, song, drama and dance

In Chapter 3, I discussed storytelling at some length, and I suggest you reread this now to bring it to mind afresh. Closely linked to stories are the performance arts such as song, dance and drama, and I will look at these in turn and also holistically, as with young children it is usually unhelpful to try to separate them.

Singing around the campfire has a long and venerable tradition, and children will enjoy making up new words to old songs. The example in the case study below is one such, and each setting will have its favourites. Songs are a sharing of ideas and feelings which help to create the togetherness of a micro-society gathered around the fire, or of a group making its way through a wood. This is a good opportunity, too, to introduce stories and songs from other cultures, ones that reflect their own indigenous links. Australia, Canada, and Scandinavia have all contributed songs to the Scouting repertoire of campfire songs, and stories such as 'Where the Forest Meets the Sea' (Baker, 1987) link modern children to older times.

 ## Case study: signature songs

My first Forest School sessions were with three- and four-year-olds and we wanted a song to swing us along on our walk to the woods. I do not remember whether it was a child or an adult who started the first line and chose the tune, but after that it was a collaborative approach as we found what we wanted to say and then made it scan. The tune was 'If you're happy and you know it clap your hands'. Each week the children then came up with a new verse as a part of the reflective process on our return. This is the first verse:

Oh, we're off to play our games in the wood
Oh, we're off to play our games in the wood
Oh, we're going to the wood, playing safely as we should
Oh, we're off to play our games in the wood

As an example of our weekly creativity, the week we were lifting worms in our play and rescuing them for the worm sanctuary, the verse came out as:

Oh, we found a lot of worms in the wood
Oh, we found a lot of worms in the wood
We found a lot of worms, and we put them in the ground
Oh, we found a lot of worms in the wood

Not perfect scansion, but it worked for us. This is an example of shared creativity, and of making a connection between an old familiar song and a new singing need. Songs can add to a sense of adventure, with no risk.

Just as children make up new songs, sometimes to old tunes, they will often dance spontaneously, just to express an excitement about an event, place or emotion. You can often read the level of excitement in a child by the number of skips per step. When you are in wilder spaces, this will take place on uneven ground and often in more unusual dance footwear, such as wellington boots. It would be a desecration of the moment to point this out to the participants, and could stifle their natural exuberance and creativity. However, once the initial euphoria has worn off, it is a good health and safety measure to look to create a dancing area that facilitates freedom of movement, and allows for foot-wear to be removed if that is desired. A dancing floor is a feature of many cultures where performances take place outside, so creating one with the children can be a positive learning experience, as well as a sign that their efforts are valued. Levels can be created if the children wish, by incorpo-rating logs into the design. This offers opportunities back in settings for links to the dances of birds such as grouse and bower birds strengthen environmental links, and in this example it creates a bridge between the cold moorlands of the north and the warm rainforests of the south.

Our consideration of the performance arts is stepping up in emotional risk terms. Songs and dance have power, but are usually of low to medium emotional risk for young children unless they link into drama. The power of children's dramatic play outdoors has been used, for example, by William Golding in his novel *Lord of the Flies* (2009 [1954]), showing how the thin line between children's understanding of fact and fiction can be crossed with consequences. The children create a tribal culture for themselves through role play and drama that culminates in the death of one of the boys, nicknamed Piggy. As I said in my introduction, creativ-ity can make the participant emotionally vulnerable, expressed here in fiction as a physical vulnerability. I will consider socio-dramatic play below, but here wish to discuss how drama can be used outdoors to express children's feelings about being in an exciting and wilder envi-ronment. The following activity gives one starting point for outdoor drama, but others may occur spontaneously as events unfold. Adult responses can scaffold the child's developing emotional literacy with their own responses and encouragement, and encourage them to share their drama if they wish to, either by replication or by recording (with photographs or video). However, not all children and not all dramas are for sharing, and it is important to recognise that it is the moment of creation that is important, not the reproduction of it.

 Activity: tell me the story

When discussing reflectively around the fire, you can help young children to express what they have seen more effectively by using their whole bodies. 'Show me what you saw' and 'Tell me the story of how you found the ...' gives permission to the children to move around and enact their sense of awe and wonder. Some children will like to do this in front of the rest of the group, while others will feel more comfortable working with you alone. Sometimes it will feel right to help them to create a narrative for their drama, and sometimes this will constrict them, but if you know your children you will know what to do for the best. Once shared, these narratives can be recreated and become part of dramas that convey to others the experience, but they will lack the power of the immediacy of the first telling. That is natural, and it will take rehearsal, adaption and recreation to put some of that magic back. It helps if you can capture some of the initial performance. We use Flip video cameras the size of a small digital camera to enable the children to take still or moving pictures. They are small enough and robust enough to take into the woods and the quality is good enough for this creative process. Created dramatic pieces can contribute to an end-of-term celebration of working outside.

Sculpture, collage and mosaic

Other forms of self-expression can involve using natural materials to create works of art. This may involve tool use, or the found ingredients may be enough for the child to make connections and see new possibilities. Figure 7.1 was found and put together by a five-year-old, and she did not need to use tools to create her image of a horse's head.

Figure 7.1 A horse's head collage

Figure 7.2   Spiral stones

It may be an idea that the child brings with them, sees on the way or finds in the wood that they wish to create or extend. In Figure 7.2, the children had seen several circles of white fungi, but the group that created this stone pattern had developed their idea from a circle to a spiral. Spirals and circles are both ancient patterns, and appear in traditional tattoos, wall paintings and artwork from many cultures. Spirals also appear in nature – sweet chestnut trees have a spiral bark, sunflowers a spiral pattern of seeds. The spiral is an essential element of the labyrinth, a winding path not to be confused with a maze. Mazes have dead-ends and you can get lost; labyrinths are a single winding route that can be therapeutic (Labyrinth Builders, 2010). This offers an opportunity for follow-up work back in the settings. However, it is important that the adult eye for a follow-up opportunity does not interfere with the creative moment for the children. Take its picture and save it for later. Another follow-up opportunity is with the art of Andy Goldsworthy, who special-ises in outdoor pieces.

My third example in this section is a sculpture. It became a sculpture because it was designated as such by one four-year-old boy. Before that, it had been a log, lying with other logs on the edge of the play space. He stood it on its end and saw something in it that was special, so he cor-doned it off with branches and called it a sculpture. For me, this comes close to some pieces of modern art in galleries that I do not understand, but I do believe that it is important to respect the creativity of others, so I offer it as an example of modern sculpture and also as a lesson that we may not always understand what we are offered by our children – what is important is that we allow it to happen and encourage it to be

Figure 7.3   Modern sculpture

respected by all in the setting. It is also an example of the richness available in the natural environment, where just by looking and interacting with the space children can find objects that communicate something special to them at a higher emotional level than words. It may be a log or a feather or a stone or a leaf, but it is a work of art by natural creation, adopted by one of us.

All of these examples involved collection for creation, rather than an alteration of the natural using tools. However, children may need to use tools for simple tasks such as shortening branches, even in art of this kind. It will be down to the practitioners to build up children's tool skills, and for some of this the practitioners themselves may need some training. Being aware of safe ways to use saws and knives is not hard, and should not be avoided because of lack of confidence. I will discuss places to seek guidance in the next chapter. Where children have a need and a purpose, they will be able to learn to use the tools they need with the level of support appropriate to their age and prior experience.

A more organised form of group creativity can be the collection of stones to form mosaics. These are lovely to make on the beach, and it is lighter to make them in situ than to carry them back to the setting to make up later. With very young children, it is easiest to start with making a pattern, as in the activity below. Once the skills have been rehearsed, however, children may wish to go on to make more complex designs that require planning and forethought, or more permanent efforts in earth rather than sand.

 ### Activity: beach group mosaics

Start by encouraging the children to collect stones and to sort them by colour. Discuss how to arrange them to form mosaics on the beach as a group. One way is to set out the groups of colours close to each other, to be almost touching. Fill in the gaps with the dominant beach colour (often grey). Another is to start with a spiral, running the colours into each other. Or a simple method is to make lines of colour butting up to each other – the children can then swap stones from one line to another to create splashes of contrasting colour. Photograph your results rather than try to take them home.

Dream catchers, hangings and other household items

Creativity can also have a decorative function, in addition to its expressive one. As well as elder beads, personal decorations can include daisy chains, chains of other flowers and leaves, and rings, bracelets and crowns made from all manner of things. For example, in Figure 7.4, I am holding a circlet made from twisting willow around itself. This can be the basis of a Dreamcatcher (see the activity on the following page) or a crown, or a smaller one can make a bracelet. We have also made these from trails of ivy, which is easier for younger children. It is poisonous, but only if you eat it, so risk-assess whether you have any nibblers in the group. The thin stems of cornus can also be coaxed into shapes, and as it has to be pruned in the spring to preserve the colours, there is usually some available at that time of year. It really is up to you and your children to experiment with what you can use. Coaxing less thin stems to bend rather than crack takes some practice, but is not hard. Just work up and down the stem in tiny steps, bending it in small amounts each time.

Figure 7.4   A willow circlet

Activity: making a wild wood dreamcatcher

Children will vary as to how much of this they can do for them-selves, but most over-twos can do some of it, making it a shared creation, and they all enjoy the finished result. Use willow or similar and twist it into a circle (most children can do this). The circle is going to be criss-crossed with string, leaving a hole in the middle. The easier way to do this is to tie the string to the edge, and then to wind it across the middle in diagonal lines. Another is to use a slip-knot to make a circle for the good dreams, and feed the string in and out of it, going around the frame on each loop. This last method is hard for children under the age of six, but produces the better effect. Decorate by hanging feathers from the bottom, and any other ornaments you can find – my children like moss, but that is to do with the nature of the wood we use. Everyone can participate in this. Tie your decorations on or weave them into the web. Hang them from the trees or take them home to hang over your bed.

Figure 7.5   A small-scale weaving frame

Another decorative item is a hanging, which may also be a mobile or a windchime, as described in Chapter 3. At its simplest, children can thread found objects such as leaves and bark onto a string, provided they can find or make holes for them, and hang them up to decorate their camps. Dreamcatchers (see activity above) are also decorative, and come from the traditions of the North American native people. The idea that they can prevent nightmares is a popular one with children; according to the traditions, the good dreams slip through the central hole while the bad dreams are caught in the web around it.

Weaving is a useful form of outdoor creativity, as while it can start on a small scale it can progress up to making shelters. The frame in Figure 7.5 is about 30 x 50 centimetres, using beech branches and string and lashed together as I learned in the Girl Guides. The children like to 'weave' (or more correctly poke) leaves and other treasures between the strings.

Larger-scale weaving is usually a cooperative task. Setting a row of branches into the ground behind the logs around the fire and weaving thinner branches in and out between them can create effective windbreaks. Once children have had the experience of making items from the natural environment, they are ready to pick up bushcraft skills as they get older that will stand them in good stead in their adult adventures. These forms of creativity help them to be open to unlikely links, make connections and see new relationships. It helps them to be innovative and create original solutions to future problems.

Dens and socio-dramatic play

At the start of the chapter, I said that self-expression facilitated outdoors has fewer boundaries, physical, psychological or emotional, than indoors and therefore can have a greater power. Given that socio-dramatic play is central to children's developing ideas about the world, themselves and their place in the world, it follows that socio-dramatic play outside has the potential to be a very powerful experience. If you talk to adults about their favourite play spaces when they were children, they usually cite an outdoor setting, and when you unpick this a little further it is often an outdoor place that cannot be seen by adults. This makes it wilder, less safe, more experimental and fluid. It is an echo of the power of 'between' places mentioned earlier, like beaches, and 'between' times, like dawn and dusk.

What can happen in these spaces is some very useful learning, not just about who we are but also about who other people are and how social groups work. Children move outwards from their caring adults a step at a time as they learn to play with other children, and to understand other adults by replicating what they have seen in their play. This happens most successfully with a progressively loosening adult scaffold, the process being in response to the interaction of experience and personality. As children's social competence grows, so they are ready to have less adult structure and further-removed supervision.

It is difficult for us as early years practitioners to facilitate socio-dramatic play that is in a secret place and that we cannot see, as it feels very risky. However, if we are flexible, we can create spaces that are wild enough to be risky enough for children to be able to experiment with ideas in their hidden play. This is often linked to the creation of dens, spaces where children can be just out of sight but not at too much risk. There are many ways for the children to make dens in wilder spaces, and also in less wild spaces, where a sheet tied to a fence or draped over a climbing frame will do very well. It can be decorated creatively wherever it is, and children will bring to it the props they need for the play they are ready for, provided we allow them to.

I have talked about my tipi, which is often the refuge of four or five interacting children. However, if children can create their own space, their play will be even richer. Figure 7.6 shows a den under construction by some young students. They have not used any ties, only propped and balanced the wood, so no damage is being done to the young trees. They have a choice at this point. They can throw a tarpaulin over their structure for an instant shelter, or they can fill in the back and sides for a more natural, and warmer, shelter. The trees they are using will be fine for a week or so like that. It is the size it is (about one and a half metres high) because of the size of the students. Smaller people make smaller dens. If children make their own, you will be unlikely to be able to enter. That is alright. They will be safe enough even if you can't see them.

Figure 7.6   A half-built den

〰 Points for practice

The relationship between the activities that take place in wilder spaces and those that take place back in settings is an interesting one, and creativity offers good examples for consideration. For example, the Rose Review (2010) asks us to encourage children to 'explore a wide range of media and materials, tools and techniques to create artworks, improvise and depict imagined worlds, and model the real world through the arts' (DCSF, 2010), and the EYFS requires 'opportunities for children to express their ideas through a wide range of types of representation' (DfES, 2007). Creativity outside naturally covers these requirements so it might be tempting for practitioners to use the output explicitly back in settings. However, transferring ideas from one to the other without due consideration is to invalidate both. The creativity that takes place outside is there *because* it is outside, and bringing it in as it is will make it look untidy, dirty, tatty and of less worth. In the same way, taking indoor creations outside makes them seem pallid, lifeless, small and uninspired. Where I have observed successful transitions has been where practitioners have made a special place for the outdoor art. This has been in the form of a photographic display, or in an outdoor gallery in the garden of the setting, or in an artistically arranged basket of artefacts. In this way, there is no attempt to measure the value of outdoor creativity against the indoor criteria, or vice versa. The transfer has been of ideas, excitement, innovation and inspiration, rather than of a literal transfer of objects.

In Forest School, we try to keep the two areas of learning separate. Different rules of behaviour and ways of being apply in the woods, and to transfer materials back without thought would be to confuse these differences for the children. We have an area where things can be put that children want to take back with them, and the advisability of doing so is always fully discussed with them, and adults who wish to take objects back do so discreetly, or come to the wood at a different time to collect them. There is a conscious consideration of not crossing lines between the two worlds without fully thinking through the psychological consequences. And just as we take care of objects we take into the woods, like magnifiers, so we take care of objects we take out of the woods.

Discussion points

With your colleagues, think about what you consider creativity to be:

- Think of something you have seen that was an innovative, flexible and adaptable idea – was it artistic? Was it creative?
- Think of something you have seen that was an original solution to a problem – was it artistic? Was it creative?
- Can you think of an example of children's art that was not creative in the sense described above?

Further reading

Craft, A. (2007) *Creativity and Possibility in the Early Years*. Available at: www.tactyc.org

Eaude, T. (2008) *Children's Spiritual, Moral, Social and Cultural Development*, 2nd edn. Exeter: Learning Matters.

Roberts, P. (2006) *Nurturing Creativity in Young People: A Report to Government to Inform Future Policy*. London: Department for Culture, Media and Sport.

Wilson, A. (2009) *Creativity in Primary Education*, 2nd edn. Exeter: Learning Matters.

Risk and Danger

Chapter objectives

In this chapter, I aim to:

- consider what reasonable risk is
- discuss what risk assessment might look like
- link risk assessment to the health and safety policies already in place in settings
- encourage practitioners to perceive risk assessment as a posi-   tive rather than a negative process
- think about the importance of non-physical risks.

Introduction

In this chapter, I aim to tackle the issues that are of concern to anyone working with children outside, those of safety and risk. Confidence in providing challenging activities, but not rash foolhardiness, should *enable* rather than *disable* adventure and risk in practice, and that confidence comes from knowledge. This knowledge is more than the adherence to a set of rules, it is about understanding and reflecting on why things happen in certain ways and the likely consequences of our actions. When it comes to working outside, it is important to keep a sense of perspective based on our knowledge of child development, our understanding of the space we are working in, plus a large dollop of common sense.

There is a sense amongst practitioners working outdoors that the tide has turned. Very cautiously and without any fanfare the advice available to the Children's Workforce is that taking risks is a necessary part of growing up, as can be seen from the readings recommended below and the references in this chapter, and that there are ways to facilitate the process. I discussed why risks are important in the introductory chapter, and throughout the book have been showing ways to do so that are appropriate not just to the age and stage of the children but also to the competence and confidence of the practitioners caring for them. As both of these last two develop, it will be possible to widen the opportunities for risk and adventure available to our children.

The EYFS (DfES, 2007) talks about 'reasonable risk taking' (on practice card 1.4), a phrase I am fond of. It means that the responsible adult has recognised the risk, examined the hazards, balanced the likelihood of an accident happening against the severity of the harm that would take place if it did happen, and taken the appropriate action. What is left is an experience where the risk is reasonable for the age and stage of the children taking part in it. This is the process of risk assessment, discussed below. For most of us working with very young children, this is really only codified common sense, as we are unlikely to be engaged in abseiling with two-year-olds. What it does do is to provide a paper trail that will evidence your preparations and considerations, particularly important in the unlikely event of anything untoward happening.

On the Learning Outside the Classroom website (www.lotc.org.uk), it states that 'a small risk of minor injury is not considered significant', but more than that would require a strategy to be in place. It does not talk about cessation immediately. To avoid the grazes, stings and bumps of childhood would be to avoid learning how to manage ourselves and our environment. The strategies adopted by settings vary, and each practitioner needs to be familiar with the requirements of their own setting. However, strategies are not once-and-for-all documents, any more than any other policy document is. They need to be reviewed regularly, and particularly after changes of legislation or advice, or after practitioners have acquired new skills that enable them to re-appraise their own practice. The review process not only facilitates modifications and alterations but also gives practitioners ownership of the policies which affect their practice. If there is no sense of ownership then there is a risk that they will be ignored, and if they are ignored by a practitioner then that person opens themselves up to accusations of unprofessional practice, or worse. In this area, ignorance is no defence.

By looking at the governmental framework supporting practitioners, we can develop a greater understanding of what needs to be in place to enable safe-enough outdoor activities. By discussing the process by which we can generate the paper trail of evidence, we can consider what the role of the responsible practitioner is in the process. And by reflecting on the nature of risk in its different forms, we can reduce our focus down to the level of the individual taking the risks, and see what it means for them, be they child or practitioner.

Health and safety (what needs to be in place)

Most settings have health and safety policies, as they are a legal require-ment. In the UK, if you do not have a robust system, the Health and Safety Executive website (www.hse.gov.uk/) is a good place to start look-ing for ideas. They have step-by-step guides, policy templates, risk assess-ment guidelines and amusing 'Myths of the Month'; the myth for March 2010 is particularly pertinent for this chapter (see Figure 8.1). With this

Great health and safety myths

The myth Risk assessment is too complicated for me to do!

The reality Carrying out a risk assessment should be straightforward. It's about focusing on real risks and hazards that cause real harm and, more importantly, taking action to control them.

 HSE   Go to www.hse.gov.uk/myth/index.htm to find out more   No 36 March 2010

Figure 8.1   HSE myth of the month, March 2010

amount of support, and the need to have policies in place anyway, the provision by settings of regimes that allow for appropriate risks and adventures should not feel too daunting.

Pages 17 and 18 of the Practice Guidance for the Early Years Foundation Stage (DfES, 2007) outline the areas that should be regularly assessed, including the outdoor spaces, and outings and trips. The ways in which this is done is left to the settings, as different strategies will be appropriate in different circumstances. Scotland's *Curriculum for Excellence through Outdoor Learning* (Learning and Teaching Scotland, 2010) provides a wealth of support, and states:

> Managing the health and safety of learners and staff in outdoor learning is vitally important but with careful planning and conduct, outdoor experiences can be both safe and stimulating. Many outdoor learning activities carry no higher risk than activities and situations faced by learners on a day-to-day basis. (LTS, 2010: 24)

When putting policies together, practitioners should remember that 'the notion of reasonableness is central to the key legislation: the Health and Safety at Work etc Act 1974 and the Occupiers' Liability Acts 1957 and 1984' (Gill, 2010). In other words, the idea that activities will be safe enough and may carry reasonable risks is central to legal requirements and policies. This is important, as it raises the issue of who is qualified to decide what is safe enough and what is reasonable. In some instances, it may not be the person who writes the policy for the setting, as was the case in the following case study.

 ## Case study: Forest School sessions

When I am taking children out of their setting for Forest School sessions, I undertake a range of risk assessments until I am happy that I am working in a safe-enough environment. I have trained to take young children into wilder spaces to undertake activities of a certain kind. The settings whose children I am taking out have agreed that I can do this because they know me, and are aware of my experience and level of qualification. They have therefore devolved to me their health and safety responsibilities for these sessions. They need evidence that they were right to do that – different settings will require different evidence, but reasonably it might include evidence that I am who I say I am, have the knowledge and skills that I claim to have, and the appropriate child protection checks have been carried out. I need the evidence that I have carried out the risk assessments, and what my decisions were in these cases. I do not

(Continued)

(Continued)

> need to give the setting my risk assessments, as they cannot be expected to have the competence to judge whether I am correct in my assessment, and indeed to offer them that opportunity would be to place them at risk of an accusation that they are incompetent to affirm or refute my judgements. But if they have correctly assessed my competence and I have correctly assessed the risks and hazards, then we are both safe enough.

The idea of the health and safety of children as being a concern for us all is in the UN Convention on the Rights of the Child (UNICEF, 1989) – in particular Articles 3 and 19, as what is stated here is the notion of the competency of staff to know what is safe enough and what constitutes reasonableness. Throughout this book, I have returned regularly to the suggestion that practitioners should receive training to support their developing outdoor provision, and this is particularly important in relation to who the person is who accepts responsibility for these reasonable risks. This may mean that the responsibility for writing the over-arching policy may lie with a practitioner who is different from the person who does the risk assessments and takes the responsibility for deciding about particular activities. In this instance, the responsibility of the manager or leader is to ensure the competence of the person undertaking the risk assessment so that they can be confident that the appropriately qualified person is making the decision.

In summary, it is up to the setting to have a policy for health and safety that includes a procedure for ensuring that a suitably qualified person assesses the risks inherent in adventurous activities. It is up to the suitably qualified person to carry out the risk assessment. It is the joint responsibility of the setting and the practitioner to ensure that they have access to the training appropriate to their need to facilitate risky and adventurous play with the children in their care. For an idea of the range of specialisms that practitioners might accrue working in outdoor settings with older children, go to www.ltscotland.org.uk/outdoorlearning/healthandsafety/activityguidance/index.asp

Risk assessments (the role of the practitioner)

An interesting first step, before carrying out a risk assessment, is to consider the concept of risk-benefit – in other words, what the benefits are of an experience balanced against an estimation of the risks of that

Figure 8.2 A climbing boulder at Needham Lake

activity. A paper written by David Ball in 2002 (Ball, 2002) looked at playgrounds in this way, and it proved to be a positive undertaking, in that he was able to make constructive recommendations that would improve the effectiveness of playgrounds as places where development through reasonable risks could take place. This was a counter to the cotton-wool culture of the previous decade, and heralded the reintroduction of risky play provision now supported by national play bodies such as Play England. The results can be seen in the play spaces being refurbished under the new county Play Strategies, for example the climbing boulder seen as Figure 8.2 at Needham Lake in Suffolk.

Once you have established the benefits of a risky activity to your children, and therefore know why you are planning to undertake it, you can start on the process of risk assessment. There are a number of equally satisfactory ways to do this, but most suggest a five-step process:

1 Identify the hazards.
2 Decide who might be harmed and how.
3 Evaluate the risks and decide on your actions or precautions.
4 Record your findings and implement them.
5 Review your risk assessment.

Identifying hazards

Hazards are the objects that interact with the children to become risks. For example, a fire is a hazard and going near it is a risk. I am looking for another hazard when I walk through a wood and look up to see if there is any dead wood caught up in branches above my head. It would be hazardous to camp underneath any such hanging dead wood as there would be a risk of it falling onto me, particularly if it is windy. Some hazards, like the first example, are obvious to any early years practitioner, who would be immediately sensitive to the interaction of children and fire. Awareness of other hazards, like the second example, comes from experience or training, or both.

Deciding who might be harmed and how

Looking at the two hazards above, we can see that the second example of hanging dead wood would be a risk to anyone underneath. The relationship between the hazard and the person does not depend upon the competence, age or experience of the person underneath. Being hit on the head by falling wood would harm anyone. This risk would be obvious to anyone aware of the danger of hanging dead wood, whatever their knowledge and experience of young children might be.

For some hazards however, like the fire mentioned first above, the perception of the level of risk involved will be affected by who might be at risk. A child who cannot be expected to have the same perception of danger by reason of their level of development or the level of their experience would be more at risk than an adult trained in lighting campfires. The accurate perception of risk here depends on the assessor being aware of three things: (1) the nature of fire; (2) the level of development of the children; and (3) what their previous experience of fire might be. The best person to be that assessor is therefore an early years practitioner trained in lighting fires outdoors, or an outdoor practitioner trained in child development, both of whom know the children in their care.

Evaluating the risks and the control measures needed

The severity of the control measures should be a response to the severity of the danger. One way of working this out is to multiply the severity of the harm by the likelihood that it will happen, and thus reaching a mathematical score which can be rated on a chart. Figure 8.3 gives one example of how to do this, while another version can be found on the HSE website (www.hse.gov.uk).

The risk rating will be affected by the controls in place. For example, if I wish to light a fire with three-year-olds, I will spend several weeks working with them until I am sure that they will follow the rules that will keep

Probability (P)

1. Highly unlikely
2. Unlikely
3. Likely

Consequence (C)

1. Slightly harmful
2. Harmful
3. Extremely harmful

Probability (P) x Consequence (C) = Risk Rating (RR)		
RR	**Description**	**Action**
1	Minimal	No action required, no documentation necessary
2	Acceptable	No extra controls necessary. Alternatives can be considered. Monitoring essential to ensure controls are maintained
3&4	Moderate	All avenues should be explored to reduce risk, and implemented within specified time limits
		If a moderate risk is associated with extremely harmful consequences then further assessment is advisable to determine more accurately the probability of harm. This can be used to evaluate the need for improved controls
6	Substantial	Activities should not start until risk has been reduced. If activity already in progress then **urgent** action should be taken
9	Unacceptable	**Activities should not start (or should be stopped) until risk has been reduced.** If this is impossible, the activity must not be carried out

Figure 8.3   Risk rating

them safe. I also have measures in place to deal with an accident, but my most effective control measure is the learning that has taken place. This will mean that while the consequences of an accident are harmful (2), the likelihood that it will happen is unlikely (2). Two times two is four, so my probability score is moderate, meaning that I can proceed with caution.

For the hanging dead wood, the consequences would also be harmful (2), but provided we do not stop under the tree and there is not a high wind, it is highly unlikely that any harm will come to us (1). Thus, we have a probability score of 2, and we can go into the wood on that route except in high winds.

Recording your findings and implementing them
Figure 8.4 shows one possible layout that I have used for recording the assessment of a piece of woodland. On the far left, I have listed the things that I liked to check, to remind me. On the far right is another reminder, of when to review each hazard. There may be things about them that will make it important to check them every time I go into the wood, or they

	Define hazard	P	C	RR	Hazard severity	Action	y/n	Review date
Site: ... Date assessed: ... Assessed by: ... Signature:								
Mobile phone signal:								
Boundaries:								
Tree layer (tree types):								
Shrub layer (types of lower branches of mature trees and small trees/large shrubs):								
Field layer (clearings, ground cover, ferns, animal habitats):								
Ground layer (mosses, fungi, leaf mould):								
Others (e.g. ponds/streams, ditches, seating, overhead power cables):								

Figure 8.4   Risk assessment sheet

may change seasonally, etc. After the identification of what the precautionary action should be, there is a tick box to say that it has been put in place.

There are plenty of alternatives to this sheet. The important thing is to ensure that you have a way of recording that you have assessed the risks and have implemented any control measures. These sheets should be kept by you for a reasonable period of time, in case you need to show evidence of your competence in the event of an accident.

Reviewing your risk assessment

It is important that your paper trail is such that if you have put a date for review, then there is a follow-up sheet to show that this review has taken place. The life of a risk assessment is only as long as the conditions stay exactly the same, which for some things may be on a single occasion.

As well as reviewing the assessment, you also need to review the process, to ensure that your methodology is the best it can be. Keeping a check on whether what you are doing complies with the law and the advice from the HSE (if you are in the UK), and is in harmony with the health and safety policies in your setting, is important. An annual review of procedures would be a sensible minimum, but factors such as additional training might cause you to take action sooner.

Non-physical risks

All of the work on risk assessments focuses on physical risks, which seem to be the main concern of most people. It is important, however, to think about the psychological and emotional risks that we ask children to take, and what control measures we put in place, often without thinking about them in these terms. For example, when a baby starts nursery at less than a year old, we are placing them at risk. At this age, the natural place for human babies for hundreds of years has been with a single main carer. In our settings, we expect the baby to be able to cope with their care being shared between a main carer at home, and at least one key worker at nursery. We put controls in place, in that we integrate the baby over time, and there are communication systems between the adults and settings. In this way, we hope to make the risk safe enough.

Now the EYFS and others, including me in this book, are suggesting that young children should be taken to other places by the people who care for them, and be exposed to the opportunities to take physical risks. We need also to consider the psychological and emotional risks of such actions. Most useful is to use Vygotsky's idea about proximal development. If the adventure we are planning is so far away from the experience of the child then the risk to them will be much greater, even if the physical demands are well within their competence. For example, in the introductory chapter, I mentioned toddlers who had only experienced tarmac, concrete and carpet under their feet. This was after a colleague had reported taking a two-year-old out to a Forest School session for the first time, and having to manage his distress at walking on earth for the first time. He was perfectly physically capable of walking on earth, but emotionally he was exposed to the risk posed by an unknown terrain. The control of 1:1 support from a trusted adult helped him to overcome the challenge and turn the risk into a new possibility, but he had to trust his carer and her support was needed. The following case study describes another example, where for one child there was a psychological risk not present for the other members of the group. It would seem from such stories that our risk assessments should also have a sheet to consider the non-physical risks of adventurous and risky play.

Case study: a step at a time

In one cohort of four- and five-year-olds going to Forest School sessions with me was a small girl with under-developed muscles and a nervous demeanour. My colleagues in the setting informed me that, whilst loving and supportive in all other ways, her mother was not keen on outdoor experiences, and the family did not go out into the countryside much, despite living in a village. It was therefore a big step for the child to go to the woods, but one we had prepared her for. She clearly wanted to join in with the other children as they played on fallen trees, climbing and jumping, but lacked the confidence. She was at risk emotionally, as if this situation had continued unmanaged her self-image and self-esteem would have been damaged by the experience. Fortunately, various adults and some other children supported her over the weeks to gain in confidence and learn to balance on logs and jump off them. Each step mastered was celebrated, and she continued to enjoy her time in the woods, developing in confidence and assurance as a result of her triumphs. Her physical skills had grown, but even more importantly her psychological coping mechanisms had been supported and had carried her through.

What would be the psychological and emotional risk in *not* taking children out for adventures and risky play? In his book 'Last Child in the Woods' (2010: 102), Richard Louv refers to research done by the Kaplans on the restorative powers of nature, noting its effects on reducing stress and helping children with disorders such as ADHD. Colin Mortlock, in his book 'The Spirit of Adventure' (2009), attempts to explain his personal journey through extreme adventures towards a better understanding of himself and his place in the world. In both books, there is a sense that man is only able to fully realise himself by engaging with the natural world in adventurous and risky ways. Certainly, it is true that through experience children come to love and respect the natural world. Such love is essential for the future of the planet, and thus so are such activities.

 Points for practice

Engaging fully with health and safety issues, rather than seeing them as irritating but necessary paperwork, offers the opportunity to see the positive in the process. By reflecting on the hazards and risks, you can focus on the beneficial outcomes of learning to manage the risks and overcoming the hazards. This should not be the task of a single person, but be a team effort to allow multiple perspectives on the issues.

This means that review regimes need to be designed to take place regularly, and to include all the stakeholders. Best practice means that the children, too, should be a part of the process. Finding ways to engage them in identifying the hazards and risks, perhaps by using cameras to take pictures of the things that they find exciting, can reveal child-eye surprises for adult perspectives. In addition, it makes the assessment process into part of the adventure, and therefore less of a chore. This relates to Article 31 of the UN Convention on the Rights of the Child (UNICEF, 1989), which states that children have the right to participate *fully* in their activities. Once they have a greater understanding of the adventures they may be engaging with, they may have valuable things to say about future activities to be planned.

 ## Discussion points

Inviting children to share their opinions and ideas will always enrich any planning process, but the younger the child the more difficult this can be. Discuss with colleagues ways to engage with children's thoughts and choices:

- Have you used IT (cameras, etc.) in any way to seek children's views?
- Have children's paintings ever revealed something valuable about their judgements?
- Have you found a way to record or note down children's opinions on given topics?

Further reading

Brock, A., Dodds, S., Jarvis, P. and Olusaga, Y. (2009) *Perspectives on Play: Learning for Life*. Harlow: Pearson Educational.

Gill, T. (2007) *No Fear: Growing Up in a Risk Averse Society*. London: Caloustie Gulbenkian Foundation.

Gill, T. (2010) *Nothing Ventured: Balancing Risks and Benefits in the Outdoors*. The English Outdoor Council. Available at: www.englishoutdoorcouncil.org

Holzman, L. and Newman, F. (2008) 'Playing in/with the ZPD', in E. Wood (ed.) *The Routledge Reader in Early Childhood Education*. London: Routledge.

Conclusion: The Role of the Adult

Chapter objectives

In this chapter, I aim to:

- draw together the main themes in the book
- reflect on the overall impact on young children
- reflect on what the implications are for practitioners
- consider ways forward for the early years sector.

The main themes in the book

The first theme that threads throughout this book is that the voices supporting the need for adventurous and risky play are multiple and various. There is a sense that there is a building pressure of recognition of an important thing (risky and adventurous play) that should be happening for children of all ages. National bodies like Play England, researchers and academics, journalists and practitioners from different parts of the Children's Workforce are referred to in the book talking and writing about the importance of risky play to children's healthy development, and about the importance of outdoor adventure to education for sustainable development (for example, Clausen, 2010). In the UK media, more television and radio programmes are offering second-hand links to nature and adventure. The EYFS and the different National Curricula in the UK are encouraging links to learning in the outdoor environment. This theme emphasises that a return to nature is a good idea for us all whatever our ages, and is very important for young children. If children do not have these experiences then there will be consequences for them as individuals, and there will be collective consequences for society. And this will inevitably involve managing the risks that such experiences involve.

These consequences are two more of the book's themes. The consequences for individual children are described in the next section, but the consequences for society can be considered first. What happens if citizens are not connected to the environment around them? As a simple example, if the perception of local people is that nettles are weeds,

then they will welcome their removal, which will have unfortunate consequences for wildlife. If the removal of nettles was replicated across a
country then pollination rates could be affected, which could affect food
production. This would affect the wealth of the nation and the well-
being of its citizens. This is simplistic, but it shows that the engagement
of individuals with, and their understanding of, nature and the environment are important when considering how to launch policies to counter
economic recession and climate change.

This relates to another theme that keeps recurring, that knowledge
equates to power. Knowledge for practitioners empowers them, giving
them confidence and allowing them to extend the range of activities
they offer. Knowledge about nature is a part of the engagement process
for adults and children alike. As an example, consider children growing
sunflowers in their settings to take home and plant out, which provide
pollen for bees and then seeds for birds. In the process, they learn about
conditions for life, about food chains and about our place in the world.
It offers opportunities to link them and their families into a heightened
awareness of the needs of bees and birds. It is also an example of the fact
that if you link young children into their environment, you are likely to
link their families in as well. If parents and carers recognise the value of
these kinds of activities then they will feel a part of a caring community.
If any of the activities are new to them, it offers them an opportunity to
further their own understanding. Even better, if you offer outdoor
opportunities to children, you may be able to strengthen relationships
with all of their families, some of whom might otherwise be more difficult to reach. There is anecdotal evidence from settings that parents who
find it a challenge to feel part of an educational community can engage
more readily when the learning is taking place outdoors, and that in that
environment they can understand what is happening more easily. This
is also true of first-generation immigrants from rural communities in
places like Bangladeshi or Roma communities, and of parents and carers
from isolated rural communities. All of these groups may also have
knowledge that they might feel able to share with the settings which
engage with the outdoor environment, thus drawing the community
together.

The process of gaining knowledge for the children may be seen to
echo my favourite theme of ontology echoing phylogeny (see Chapter
1). This is the notion that children naturally develop in ways similar to
the development of our species. Our species, as they moved out of Africa
and integrated with the Neanderthals that preceded them, were firstly
hunter-gatherers and then agriculturalists. Our bodies developed in
response to those early needs, and therefore also need to be outside and
exercising, and so our children need to be able to be outside stretching
and developing their physical skills. Playing outside can replicate other

behaviours that have echoes from earlier times, and integrate them into modern learning in ways that feel harmonious and in tune with our underlying instincts. For example, a group of four-year-olds and I found a dead snake near the pond we pass on the way to their wood. It had been partially eaten, and left. We were not sure whether it was a slow-worm or a grass snake, so we took it back to the setting and used the internet to identify it. The children were using their skills of observation and their computer skills in equal balance, and learning about death (and decay – it smelt!) and predation and species identification, not to mention how to pick up a dead animal safely and the importance of washing our hands afterwards.

Activities of this kind give a sense of continuity over time, but the references and readings in the book also give a sense that our concerns about the importance of adventurous play outdoors has a continuity over space. Early years workers across the world are concerned that we should not be disconnecting children from their environments as they grow and learn, and where there is a fear that this has already happened that we should work to reconnect them. Academics and practitioners in different countries are identifying ways to do this that have clear commonalities for our youngest children, around focusing on being child-initiated and led, and around encompassing risk and extending the boundaries of play. What is interesting is that this focus on the outdoors and on natural resources is not new. The works of pioneers from Pestalozzi to Malaguzzi via Steiner, the MacMillan sisters and others, all emphasised the importance of natural materials, of outdoor spaces and of connecting with the environment through concrete interactions.

Recognising the global nature of the move towards more adventurous and risky outdoor play is also to recognise that modern communication is making the world a smaller place. We are able to see good practice in many different places, and we are also more aware of the many threats to the environment and to the well-being of citizens in other communities across the globe than was previously possible. We are more aware that our local actions can have global effects, and it is important that our children grow up with this sense of global kinship. A good example is the work done by the Green Light Trust, who have strong links with tribal people in the rainforests of Papua New Guinea, and who were asked by the locals there how they protected the forests in Suffolk. At the time, almost the only forests left in Suffolk were the pine plantations belonging to the Forestry Commission, other remnants of our Palaeolithic past being relegated to small pockets of woodland here and there. The charity started their work in their own village, establishing a community wood that has grown and spread over the subsequent 20 or more years, and still each child attending the school plants an acorn or other indigenous tree seed in their reception year, and plants their tree in the wood when they move up to secondary school. Over a 100 oth[...] in the UK have followed this lead, and many have for[...] other groups across the world, often where there are[...] issues to be confronted. Living and learning in these[...] local children a sense of a connection both with nature[...] peoples of the world.

It is not just rural communities that can encourage wilder and more adventurous play. Another theme in the book has been about access through ingenuity, recognising where urban settings have used the resources that they can access to enable children's regular wilder play, as well as occasional outings to other places such as beaches and forests. There are accounts and pictures from parks and gardens in large conurbations where practitioners have recognised that for very young children, adventure can be found in small spaces or in the overlooked corners of otherwise manicured parks. A good example of this is the Chelsea Open Air Nursery School in London, where space is recognised to be a cube, as can be seen in on page 118.

The impact of adventurous play provision on young children

Throughout the book is the repeated exhortation that being given opportunities to challenge themselves and thus to develop their physical skills is important for young children. Different sources refer to its importance in countering obesity, an important first world issue, as well as establishing habits of healthy living that will last into adulthood. There are also references to the benefits of integrating learning with vigorous outdoor experiences, particularly for boys who need opportunities for rough and tumble as all young male animals do. This will be addressed again in Appendix 2, offering suggestions for curriculum mapping for practitioners.

Learning to manage risk and adventure has important cognitive benefits, not just in increasing knowledge but also in developing personality traits such as teamworking skills, motivation, concentration and perseverance. The projects monitored by the Forestry Commission (O'Brien and Murray, 2007) provide evidence of these developing dispositions, which Lucas and Claxton (2010) identify as being so important for successful learning. These attitudes when learned young last longest, in the same way as the habits of health in the previous paragraph, which is why it is so important to make an early start. When the brain is at its most plastic and malleable, and developing at its fastest rate, is the time to establish the dispositions to support children through the whole of their lives. Most of this time occurs before formal schooling starts, so it

Figure 1   Chelsea Open Air Nursery School

is the responsibility of early years practitioners to see that the right opportunities exist.

These dispositions are in part emotional, as the mastery of risky and adventurous activities builds resilience. But another important theme running through the book is about our emotional responses to the wonders of nature, valuing our sense of awe and wonder. Adults working with older children and young people describe this happening when mountains are conquered and expeditions reach their goals. With young children, the awe and wonder is in moments, places and objects that are more familiar to the adults with them, but are no less precious. A sunset, a rock pool, a bird singing, a flower where there wasn't one last week, each can trigger a response in a child that creates a special moment that will stay with them forever. Every one of us has that child within us, and those of us who have them beside us, too, have the best helpers for rediscovering our own inner child. Watching their responses as they balance on a log for the first time, or discover a nest in a bush, or peer over a rock can give us, too, a sense of the mystery of life and our place in the natural world. The spiritual aspect of outdoor learning is important to adults and children. When I take groups out to take part in Forest School sessions, it is not only the children who are refreshed. These are not moments to be rushed, and often outdoor adventures do not have the same time constraints on them as indoor experiences, so the opportunity is there.

The implications for practitioners

Becoming aware of the importance of extending outdoor experiences to make them riskier and more adventurous can be daunting. But it is important to remember two things. First is the old adage that you can eat a whole elephant if you do so one mouthful at a time. The elephant of adventurous play can be eaten in very small mouthfuls, and you will be amazed at how much you can eat. Second is the knowledge that what is risky for a very small child is not very risky for you. Start with where your children are now and progress together. But the first implication of this book is that practitioners do need to develop more adventurous opportunities for the children in their care, for all the reasons discussed above.

In the discussion sections at the end of each chapter, I have put down ideas to mull over. They will help you to develop your team, and early years practitioners are always part of a team, even if the team is two – you and the main carer. Do not expect to be able to do everything yourself – develop skill-sets that can be shared, and that will help you to build your confidence. Seek out others in similar situations for mutual support, and local experts for ideas and leadership. The second implication of the book is that every setting has the same imperative, so there are practitioners out there to link up with.

In the Points for practice section of each chapter, I have suggested ways to progress and to start taking action. It has been exciting to see the effects on local play provision in the UK of the government's Play Builder scheme, which was built around the need to address the lack of 'safe, stimulating and challenging places for children and young people to go' (Rogers et al., 2009). This is local and real action that you can look out for, and that might help your settings. For example, at Needham Lake, a park in Suffolk, they have built a climbing boulder to offer children of all ages the opportunity to climb a 'natural' rock, and work out their own level of challenge, in a landscape otherwise devoid of such opportunities (see Figure 8.2) and two 'tree trunk' tunnels (see Figure 2 on page 120). Not all settings have the space or the funds to create such an opportunity, but if such exists locally then the need is to find a way to get to it, not to recreate it. The third imperative is therefore not just to take action but to take flexible, adaptable and opportunistic actions that best suit your children and your settings.

As you develop your ideas, you will find a need for tools, ones that are real but simple enough for you and your children. However, there is a

Figure 2   Tree trunk tunnels at Needham Lake

lot you can do without tools, and it is not until you have tried out a few ideas that you will know which tools work for you. So your last imperative is to ensure that you have the tools that you need, but to wait until you know what you really need.

The way forward

As you develop your adventurous projects, you will need to give consideration to using different methods for observations, assessments and recording. It is important to ensure that you have records of the development of individual children, as always, but it is equally important to record the effects of changes in ways of doing things for the whole setting. Practitioners I have helped to start Forest School sessions have often said that they wish that they had kept better records as evidence of the effects of working outside on their children. Not to have bullied them into doing so was an oversight on my part that I am redressing here. Keep records, or you will not have the evidence to use when you reflect on and evaluate your practice.

Another good reason for keeping observational records is that you will find that children working outside do not need your constant intervention, but your sensitive and occasional intervention. You will not know when it is the right time if you are not observing, and it will stop you feeling guilty about just watching if you feel that you are doing something. Watching not doing is still working. As Trisha Maynard (2007) found, this is very hard for teachers, but it is really important if children are going to be able to really find out and learn about risk and adventure.

Further reading

Ashton, E. et al. (2009) *Play and Playfulness: Professional Support Document.* University of New Brunswick: Early Childhood Centre.

Ouvry, M. (2003) *Exercising Muscles and Minds.* London: National Children's Bureau.

Pretty, J. et al. (2009) *Nature, Childhood, Health and Life Pathways.* Colchester: University of Essex. Available at: www.essex.ac.uk/ces/occasionalpapers/Nature%20 Childhood%20and%20Health%20iCES%20Occ%20Paper%202009-2%20FINAL. pdf (accessed 19 May 2010).

Appendix 1: Useful Resources

Organisations

British Conservation Trust Volunteers (BCTV) – a UK charity providing resources, equipment and training as well as undertaking environmental and conservation work themselves. A rich source of support, advice and expertise.
BCTV, Sedum House, Mallard Way, Doncaster DN4 8DB
T: 01302 388 883
F: 01302 311 531
www.btcv.org.uk

Environmental Education Departments – most counties in the UK have an environmental education department, often a part of the education department. Searching your county council's website can give you access to useful expertise.

Facebook – there is at least one support group, Forest School Leaders UK, and I expect more will spring up.

Forest Education Initiative – part of the UK Forestry Commission, this is the wing that has taken on the support of Forest School. It has a register of all the Cluster Groups that have formed around the country, and to which it can offer support and direction towards funding streams. It has developed a Quality Assurance scheme for Forest School and can help identify training providers. It lists resources for activities on its website: www.foresteducation.org

England: Susannah Podmore, FEI Forestry Commission, Whitcliffe, Ludlow, Shropshire SY8 2HD T: 07768 036542

Scotland: Bonnie Maggio, FEI Silvan House, 231 Corstorphine Rd, Edinburgh EH12 7AT T: 01738 771034

Wales South East: Carol Travers, FEI c/o Forestry Commission Wales, Cantref Court, Brecon Road, Abergavenny NP7 7AX T: 0845 604 0845

Wales North & Mid: Kim Burnham, FEI c/o Forestry Commission Wales, Gwydr Uchaf, Llanrwst, Conwy LL24 0DE T: 0845 604 0845

Wales South & West: Owen Thurgate, FEI c/o Forestry Commission Wales, Llanymddyfri Forest District, Llanfair Rd, Llandovery, Carmarthenshire SA20 0AL T: 0845 604 0845

Green Light Trust – a UK environmental charity which works with schools, settings and communities in many different ways, including Community Wild Spaces and Forest School.
Green Light Trust, The Foundry, Bury Road, Lawshall, Bury St Edmunds, Suffolk IP29 4PJ T: 01284 830829 F: 01284 830845
www.greenlighttrust.org

Institute for Outdoor Learning – represents many different kinds of outdoor learning and includes special interest groups for Forest School and Bushcraft which can help to identify training providers, practitioners and skills development opportunities.
Warwick Mill Business Centre, Warwick Bridge, Carlisle, Cumbria, CA4 8RR T: 01228 564580 F: 01228 564581
www.outdoor-learning.org

KIDS National Development Department – National Training and Inclusion Projects including the Playwork Inclusion Project – a charity supporting the inclusion of children with particular needs in outdoor play.
6 Aztec Row, Berners Road, London N1 0PW
T: 020 7359 3073
www.kids.org.uk

Learning Through Landscapes – a leading charity for developing outdoor learning spaces in schools and settings:

England: 3rd Floor Southside Offices, The Law Courts, Winchester, Hampshire SO23 9DL T: 01962 846258 www.ltl.org.uk

Scotland: Grounds for Learning, Inglewood House, Alloa, Clackmannanshire FK10 2HU T: 01259 220 887 www.gflscotland.org.uk

Wales: LTL Cymru, Maindy House, 96 Whitchurch Road, Cardiff CF14 3LY T: 02920 227929 www.ltl-cymru.org.uk

National Trust – a UK property protecting over 350 sites of interest including many gardens and grounds that can be accessible to groups of children.
The National Trust, PO Box 39, Warrington WA5 7WD
T: 0844 800 1895 F: 0844 800 4642
www.nationaltrust.org.uk

Outdoor Education Centres – across the UK there are many centres, some with residential provision, some of whom are privately owned and some owned by local government agencies. Many run classes that can be of interest to practitioners for CPD, or for their children. Most belong to the Institute for Outdoor Learning (see entry above), and can be found via their website, or by Googling to find those local to you.

Royal Horticultural Society (RHS) – a leading horticultural charity which works with some UK universities on their 'learning outside the classroom' training, and which offers support to schools and settings interested in getting children involved in gardening. Head Office: 80 Vincent Square, London SW1P 2PE
T: 0845 260 5000
www.rhs.org.uk

RHS gardens: Harlow Carr: 01423 565418 Hyde Hall: 01245 400256 Rosemoor: 01805 624067 Wisley: 0845 260 9000

Wilderness Foundation – 'Dedicated to preserving the last of the world's wild places, the Wilderness Foundation UK nurtures understanding of the value of wilderness to the health of the individual, society and the planet'. The charity has programmes under three banners: (1) Education and Leadership, (2) Health and Well-being, Peace and Reconciliation and (3) Wilderness Therapy.
Wilderness Foundation UK, 47–49 Main Road, Broomfield, Chelmsford, Essex CM1 7BU
T: 01245 443073 F: 01245 445035
www.wildernessfoundation.org.uk

Wildlife Trusts – in the UK, there is a network of 47 Wildlife Trusts. These manage reserves which usually have public access and work with schools and settings to provide a range of services, which may include Forest School sessions. They also have junior membership which gives access to useful publications. In England and Wales, there is almost one per county, while Scotland and Northern Ireland have one each.
Head Office: The Kiln, Waterside, Mather Road, Newark, Nottinghamshire NG24 1WT
T: 01636 677711 F: 01636 670001
www.wildlifetrusts.org

Woodcraft Folk – 'The Woodcraft Folk is an educational movement for children and young people, which aims to develop self confidence and activity in society, with the aim of building a world based on equality, friendship, peace and co-operation'. Formed at the turn of the twentieth

century and supported by prominent members of the socialist movement including the MacMillan sisters, it has links with North American
native people. It is a youth movement with a strong environmental
emphasis, and a section (Woodchips) for the under sixes.
Head Office: Woodcraft Folk, Units 9/10, 83 Crampton Street, London
SE17 3BF
T: 020 7703 4173 F: 020 7358 6370
www.woodcraft.org.uk

Suppliers

Community Playthings: ethically sourced, very robust wooden play
equipment from the USA.
UK contact: Community Playthings, Robertsbridge, East Sussex TN32
5DR
T: 0800 387 457 F: 0800 387 531
www.communityplaythings.com

EarthCraftuk Ltd: members of the Institute for Outdoor Learning, and
of the Bushcraft and Forest School Special Interest Groups. Courses for
CPD, equipment, books, etc. PO Box 402, Deal, Kent CT14 4AD
T: 01304 612911
www.earthcraftuk.com

Insect Lore: resources for outdoor learning in settings, including kits for
hatching butterflies – aimed at the older end of the Foundation Stage
upwards.
Unit 11, Indian Queens Trading Estate, Warren Road, Indian Queens,
Cornwall TR9 6TL
T: 01726 860 273 F: 01726 862 847
www. insectlore-europe.com

Mindstretchers Ltd: clothing and equipment for your children, training
and books for your staff, including visits to their nature kindergartens.
The Warehouse, Rossie Place, Auchterarder, Perthshire PH3 1AJ
T: 01764 664409 F: 01764 660728
www.mindstretchers.co.uk

Muddy Puddles: suppliers of a wide range of outdoor clothing for all
sizes of children.
Hingston Farm, Bigbury, Kingsbridge, Devon TQ7 4BE
T: 0844 557 4945
www.muddypuddles.com

Outdoor Explorers: resources to support outdoor learning, particularly gardening.
Commotion Group, Commotion House, Morley Road, Tonbridge, Kent TN9 1RA
T: 01732 225850
www.reflectionsonlearning.co.uk

Puddlejumpers: outdoor clothing for babies to 10-year-olds. Harley Grange, Earl Sterndale, Buxton SK17 OEP
T: 01298 83812
www.puddlejumpers.co.uk

Woodland Survival Crafts Ltd: member of the Institute for Outdoor Learning, and of the Bushcraft Special Interest Groups courses and support about bushcraft skills.
Windlehill Farm, Sutton on the Hill, Ashbourne, Derbyshire DE6 5JH
T: 01283 730851 M: 07736 225035 www.woodlandsurvivalcrafts.com

Places to visit (at a charge) for inspiration

Bridgwater College Children's Centre,
Bridgwater College, Bath Road, Bridgwater, Somerset TA6 4PZ
T: 01278 455464 F: 01278 444363
Children's Centre Direct Line: 01278 441270 www.bridgwater.ac.uk
Bishops Wood Environmental Centre Crossway Green, Stourport, Worcs. DY13 9SE T: 01299 250513 F: 01299 250131 www.bishopswoodcentre. org.uk

Chelsea Open Air Nursery School and Children's Centre
51 Glebe Place, London SW3 5JE
T: 020 7352 8374 F: 020 7376 8350 www.coans.rbkc.sch.uk

Nature Kindergartens
Mindstretchers Ltd, The Warehouse, Rossie Place, Auchterarder, Perthshire PH3 1AJ
T: 01764 664409 F: 01764 660728
www.mindstretchers.co.uk

Appendix 2: Curriculum Links

In this appendix, I have taken one activity from each chapter (except Chapter 8, where all the activities were for adults) and shown how it maps to the statutory early years curricula in the UK. I have only focused on one or two curriculum areas for each activity, but this does not mean that they do not cover other areas, merely that this is not the main focus that I have homed in on. You could legitimately decide to use the same activity but focus on different outcomes.

Chapter 1   Activity: muddy face (EYFS curriculum areas – Communication, Language and Literacy; Creativity)

Chapter 2   Activity: smell pots (EYFS curriculum areas – Creativity; Knowledge and Understanding of the World)

Chapter 3   Activity: wild wood wind chimes (EYFS curriculum areas – Problem Solving, Reasoning and Numeracy; Physical Development)

Chapter 4   Activity: engaging the children in collecting material to burn (EYFS curriculum areas – Personal, Social and Emotional; Knowledge and Understanding of the World)

Chapter 5   Activity: making a tipi (EYFS curriculum areas – Personal, Social and Emotional; Problem Solving, Reasoning and Numeracy)

Chapter 6   Activity: experimenting with tracks and signs (EYFS curriculum areas – Knowledge and Understanding of the World; Physical Development)

Chapter 7   Activity: making a wild wood dreamcatcher (EYFS curriculum areas – Creativity; Communication, Language and Literacy)

Chapter 1 Activity: muddy face

There are variations on this activity, so it should be adapted to suit the ages and stages of the children, and developed along their lines of interest. In its simplest form, mud or earth is collected in a bucket – if stones can be avoided this is a good thing. Water is added to create a stiff paste – too much, and the faces will slide; too little, and they won't stick.

Take a handful of the paste, knead it in your hand, and then slap it onto a tree. You can use a fence post, but the rougher surfaces give a better adhesion. Find sticks, leaves, etc., to turn the blobs into faces. You can use these to start stories, or however you wish.

English Early Years Foundation Stage 0–5-year-olds	Welsh Foundation Phase 3–7-year-olds	Scottish Curriculum for Excellence (Early Years 3–5-year-olds)
Communication, Language and Literacy: opportunities to interact, tell and respond to stories, extend vocabulary, use words to clarify thinking	Language, Literacy and Communication Skills: an experience of a stimulus to story and poetry, that will extend vocabulary	Literacy and English: an opportunity to extend and enrich vocabulary through listening and talking, exploring events and characters in stories and sharing thoughts in different ways
Creativity: a provision of support for curiosity, exploration and play, in order to help with using imagination while exploring texture, shape and form	Creativity: a provision of support to develop understanding and use of texture, shape and form, and skills in designing, modelling and modification	Expressive Arts: a provision of support to develop ways to create images and objects using a variety of materials

Chapter 2 Activity: smell pots

Equip your children with something like an empty yoghurt pot, and send them to collect samples from their favourite bush/tree/plant/flower with cautions about protecting the plant by only picking small amounts. Encourage them to add small amounts of water to their pots and mash up the contents to release the natural oils into the water. Compare the scents. Leave them for a day and smell how they change.

Extension activities include the blending of natural perfumes and the mixing of potions for imaginative play. Discussions about not tasting these are advised!

English Early Years Foundation Stage 0–5-year-olds	Welsh Foundation Phase 3–7-year-olds	Scottish Curriculum for Excellence Early Years 3–5-year-olds
Creativity: an opportunity to respond to smell, touch and vision, communicating through experimentation with a range of materials	Creativity: an opportunity to mix and combine materials to create own objects, communicating through experimentation with a range of materials	Sciences: an opportunity to explore different materials and to share reasons for selecting materials for different purposes
Knowledge and Understanding of the World: an opportunity to investigate objects and materials in the natural world, and find out about how things change	Knowledge and Understanding of the World: an opportunity to explore and experiment, thinking about what might happen, making comparisons and identifying similarities and differences	Sciences: an opportunity to develop curiosity and understanding of the environment and our place in the living, material and physical world

Chapter 3 Activity: wild wood wind chimes

Select a stick to be the hanger, and tie a string to either end. While the children are making the chimes, they can hang this from a low branch. Ask them to select items that make a sound when they are tapped together. Hollow objects will make louder sounds. Tie a string to each and suspend them from the stick close together and at the same height – it will depend on the age and experience of your children as to how much of the tying they can manage. Now they can suspend their creations where they like, and listen to the sounds they make when the wind blows on them.

English Early Years Foundation Stage 0–5-year-olds	Welsh Foundation Phase 3–7-year-olds	Scottish Curriculum for Excellence Early Years 3–5-year-olds
Problem Solving, Reasoning and Numeracy: a context in which to explore and compare the qualities of objects in terms of their shape, size and weight, and to describe relational positions	Mathematical Development: an opportunity to play with shapes, and develop their understanding of position and movement	Numeracy and Mathematics: a context in which to investigate objects and shapes and to sort, describe and be creative with them
Physical Development: an opportunity to improve skills of coordination, control and manipulation	Physical Development: an opportunity to improve skills of coordination, control and manipulation	Health and Well-being: an opportunity to move and explore how to manage and control bodies, and find out how to use and share space

Chapter 4 Activity: engaging the children in collecting material to burn

The first material you will need to start your fire will be tinder, and it may be advisable to bring your own in a sealed container, to ensure success. The ultimate cheat is a couple of cotton wool balls with just a light smear of Vaseline – they will need to be teased out to let the air through. However, do send the children to look for the driest materials to make natural tinder, such as dead (dry) grass and leaves, the fluffy seeds from rosebay willowherb and wild clematis. If you are in a hazel wood, you may find 'King Alfred's Cakes', a hard black fungus stuck to the trees, which is like charcoal to burn. Next you will need kindling, usually thin dead wood. The best dead wood is that which is 'hanging', i.e. caught up in other vegetation above ground level, as there it will be at its driest. Make separate piles beside the fire site of the different sizes. Start with twigs that are as thin as a match and as long as the children's hands. Describing the wood to collect in these terms helps the children to sort by suitable size, as you can show them what you mean. Next you need twigs as thick as the children's little fingers and as long as their forearms. Ask them to test the wood by snapping it – it is only dry enough if it snaps easily and cleanly. Lastly you will need fuel, which is thicker wood. The children may become very enthusiastic at this stage, and find long pieces of dead branches that they struggle to drag back to camp, which will give you the opportunity to demonstrate the use of suitable tools to cut them into useable sizes. This wood will need to be dry to start with, but a well-established fire will burn greener wood, although that will create more smoke. Keep your fuel stacked to one side and do not feed the fire with more than you need, or it will be difficult to put out.

English Early Years Foundation Stage 0–5-year-olds	Welsh Foundation Phase 3–7-year-olds	Scottish Curriculum for Excellence Early Years 3–5-year-olds
Personal, Social and Emotional: the chance to work in a group and to develop self-control, risk awareness and respect	Personal and Social Development, Well-being and Cultural Diversity: an opportunity to develop an understanding of the behavioural expectations of the setting	Religious and Moral Education: an opportunity to develop an understanding of what is fair and unfair and the importance of caring for, sharing and cooperating with others
Knowledge and Understanding of the World: a chance to explore the natural world and refine observational skills	Knowledge and Understanding of the World: a chance to explore the natural world and refine observational skills, sorting and grouping	Technologies: a chance to develop practical skills, selecting and working with a range of materials and tools

Chapter 5 Activity: making a tipi

This involves pairs of children collecting three poles and arranging them ready to tie, in threes spreading the legs of the tent when tied, in pairs adding in extra poles, then two to four children wrapping tarpaulin around and pegging it down. Using a very elderly sewing machine and a cheap tarpaulin from a warehouse of outdoor goods, I cut out triangles from one side of the rectangle and inserted them into the other side to create a shape that could be wrapped around a cone of sticks. I attached ties to the top (short) side, and peg loops to the bottom (long) side. Figure 5.3 shows the end result, which many of you will be able to improve on, but it has worked for groups with me. Once you have constructed your own cover, you can involve the children. You will need six poles of similar lengths – which will depend on the size of the tarpaulin, but are likely to be between two and three metres in length, and a piece of rope to tie around the top. When I am running Forest School sessions, I hide them near the base camp between sessions. The children and I agreed that they would need to carry one pole between two, not because they are heavy but because they are likely to swing around and clonk others when carried by one child. Balance three in a tripod and tie once – the tying has to be done by an adult because of the height. Then place the other three in between them, and tie securely. Wrap the cover around the poles, tie it and peg it down. In my experience, once three- and four-year-olds have been shown how to do this twice, they will take over getting it set up, apart from tying the top.

English Early Years Foundation Stage 0–5-year-olds	Welsh Foundation Phase 3–7-year-olds	Scottish Curriculum for Excellence Early Years 3–5-year-olds
Personal, Social and Emotional: a chance to develop social skills, form good relationships, and develop independence	Personal and Social Development, Well-being and Cultural Diversity: a chance to Form relationships and feel confident to play and work cooperatively	Social Studies: a chance to make choices about where I work, how I work and who I work with
Problem Solving, Reasoning and Numeracy: a practical counting activity, involving judgements about length and size	Mathematical Development: an opportunity to compare and match objects in terms of length, to calculate mentally and investigate patterns	Numeracy and Mathematics: a practical counting activity, developing a sense of size and amount by observing, exploring, using and communicating with others about things in the world

Chapter 6 Activity: experimenting with tracks and signs

When walking in wilder areas, or indeed observing any muddy patch, children will be able to see the tracks left by the animals and birds that share their environment, but that they might otherwise be unaware of. Figure 6.3 shows pheasant tracks which are large, clear and frequent in rural areas. Small, clear and frequent are the dainty pairs of dots of deer tracks. In urban areas, the bird prints may be smaller, and the animal prints, such as dogs and cats, larger. It is fun to collect these – they can be recorded (depending on the solidity of the mud) by rubbings, taking plaster casts, drawings and photographs. Children may also look out for other signs of animals passing, such as hairs caught on twigs and fences. These can then be researched back in the settings, and children can work out their possible routes of travel, and possible reasons for those routes. A game between two teams can then take place, where one side lays a track for the others to follow. I played this as a Girl Guide, leaving arrows of twigs on the ground, and coloured cottons on twigs. Children can agree their own signals for each other, and the followers need to wait ten minutes for the trailblazers to start. When they catch them up, the roles are reversed. If they fail to catch them, the conventional sign for 'gone home' is a ring of stones with one in the middle. This game addresses the targets for the personal, social and emotional (PSE) curriculum, as well as linking to geography, biology and history (in the stories of tracking by hunters).

English Early Years Foundation Stage 0–5-year-olds	Welsh Foundation Phase 3–7-year-olds	Scottish Curriculum for Excellence Early Years 3–5-year-olds
Knowledge and Understanding of the World: a chance to use observations of the natural environment to construct messages for each other, and an opportunity to discuss other cultures	Knowledge and Understanding of the World: an opportunity to learn about distance, direction and routes, to identify natural features and to discuss other cultures	Social Studies: an opportunity to learn how to locate, explore and link features and places locally and further afield, to explore and discover the interesting features of local environments to develop an awareness of the world
Physical Development: involves travelling and moving safely through the natural world	Physical Development: an opportunity to become proficient at travelling through the natural world	Health and Well-being: an opportunity to demonstrate how to travel safely, to make friends and to be part of a group

Chapter 7 Activity: making a wild wood dreamcatcher

Twist whips of willow, cornus or ivy into a circle. Use secateurs under supervision if appropriate. Decide how to use it – if making a dreamcatcher, work with an adult to cut and tie strings, then decorate as required with found objects. Children will vary as to how much of this they can do for themselves, but most over-twos can do some of it, making it a shared creation, and they all enjoy the finished result. Use willow or similar and twist it into a circle (most children can do this). The circle is going to be criss-crossed with string, leaving a hole in the middle. The easier way to do this is to tie the string to the edge, and then to wind it across the middle in diagonal lines. Another is to use a slip-knot to make a circle for the good dreams, and feed the string in and out of it, going around the frame on each loop. This last method is hard for children under the age of six, but produces the better effect. Decorate by hanging feathers from the bottom, and any other ornaments you can find – my children like moss, but that is to do with the nature of the wood we use. Everyone can participate in this. Tie your decorations on or weave them into the web. Hang them from the trees or take them home to hang over your bed.

English Early Years Foundation Stage 0–5-year-olds	Welsh Foundation Phase 3–7-year-olds	Scottish Curriculum for Excellence Early Years 3–5-year-olds
Creativity: an exploration of 3D materials to create and to communicate ideas, thoughts and feelings	Creativity: an exploration of 3D materials to create and to communicate ideas, thoughts and feelings, working in a small group	Expressive Arts: an opportunity to discover and choose ways to create images and objects using a variety of materials; expressing and communicating ideas, thoughts and feelings through activities within art and design
Communication, Language and Literacy: an interactive activity, culminating in an opportunity to create a narrative	Language, Literacy and Communication Skills: an interactive activity with adults and other children giving the opportunity to communicate thoughts, ideas and feelings	Literacy and English: an interactive activity exploring and choosing stories to listen to and share, exploring events and characters, and sharing thoughts

References

Alexander, R.J. (2009a) *Towards a New Primary Curriculum: a Report from the Cambridge Primary Review. Part 1: The Past and Present*. Cambridge: University of Cambridge Faculty of Education.

Alexander, R.J. (2009b) *Towards a New Primary Curriculum: a Report from the Cambridge Primary Review. Part 2: The Future*. Cambridge: University of Cambridge Faculty of Education.

Ashton, E., Stewart, K., Hurt, A., Nason, P. and Scheffel, T-L. (2009) *Play and Playfulness: Professional Support Document*. University of New Brunswick: Early Childhood Centre.

Baker, J. (1987) *Where the Forest Meets the Sea*. London: Walker Books.

Ball, D. (2002) *Playgrounds: Risks, Benefits and Choices*. Norwich: HMSO.

Ball, D., Gill, T. and Spiegal, B. (2008) *Managing Risk in Play Provision: Implementation Guide*. Nottingham: DCSF.

Barron, P. (2009) *Games, Ideas and Activities for Learning Outside the Primary Classroom*. Harlow: Pearson Education Ltd.

Brock, A., Dodds, S., Jarvis, P. and Olusaga, Y. (2009) *Perspectives on Play: Learning for Life*. Harlow: Pearson Educational.

Burke, K.A., Hand, B., Poock, J. and Greenbowe, T. (2005) 'Using the science writing heuristic: Training Chemistry Teaching Assistants', *Journal of College Science Teaching*, 35(2): 36.

Callaway, G. (2005) *The Early Years Curriculum: A View From Outdoors*. London: David Fulton.

Canning, N. (2009) 'Empowering communities through inspirational leadership', in A. Robins and S. Callan (eds) *Managing Early Years Settings*. London: Sage.

Carr, M. (2001) *Assessment in Early Childhood Settings*. London: Sage.

Casey, T. (2007) *Environments for Outdoor Play: A Practical Guide to Making Space for Children*. London: Paul Chapman.

Clark, A. (2007) 'Views from inside the shed: young children's perspectives of the outdoor environment', *Education 3–13: International Journal of Primary, Elementary and Early Years Education*, 35(4): 349–63.

Clausen, R. (2010) 'Teaching sustainability as if your life depended on it: a photo essay of Fort Lewis College's Ecology and Society Field School', *The Journal of Sustainability Education*, 9 May. Available at: www.journalofsustainability education.org/wordpress/ (accessed 22 May 2010).

Conway, M. (2008) 'Playwork principles', in F. Brown and C. Taylor (eds) *Foundations of Playwork*. Maidenhead: Open University Press.

Craft, A. (2007) *Creativity and Possibility in the Early Years*. Available at: www. tactyc.org (accessed 13 May 2010).

Danks, F. and Schofield, J. (2009) *Go Wild: 101 Things To Do Before You Grow Up*. London: Frances Lincoln.

DCSF (2008) *The Play Strategy*. Nottingham: HMSO.

DCSF (2010) *The National Curriculum Primary Handbook*. Coventry: QCDA.

DfES (2006) *Learning Outside the Classroom Manifesto*. Nottingham: HMSO (and www.lotc.org.uk).

DfES (2007) *The Early Years Foundation Stage*. Nottingham: HMSO.

Duffy, B. (2006) *Supporting Creativity and Imagination in the Early Years*. Maidenhead: Open University Press.

Eaude, T. (2008) *Children's Spiritual, Moral, Social and Cultural Development*, 2nd edn. Exeter: Learning Matters.

Ellaway, A., Kirk, A., Macintyre, S. and Mutrie, N. (2007) 'Nowhere to play? The relationship between the location of outdoor play areas and deprivation in Glasgow', *Health and Place*, 13(2): 557–61.

Elliott, S. and Davis, J. (2004) 'Mud pies and daisy chains: connecting young children and nature', *Every Child*, 10 (4). Available from www.earlychildhood australia.org.au (accessed 13 March 2010).

Gill, T. (2007) *No Fear: Growing Up in a Risk Averse Society*. London: Caloustie Gulbenkian Foundation.

Gill, T. (2010) *Nothing Ventured: Balancing Risks and Benefits in the Outdoors*. The English Outdoor Council. Available at: www.englishoutdoorcouncil.org

Golding, W. (2009 [1954]) *Lord of the Flies*. London: Faber Firsts.

Goldschmied, E. and Jackson, S. (2004) *People Under Three*, 2nd edn. Abingdon: Routledge.

Health and Safety Executive (HSE) (2010) *Myths of the Month: February 2010*. Available at: www.hse.gov.uk (accessed 31 March 2010).

Holzman, L. and Newman, F. (2008) 'Playing in/with the ZPD', in E. Wood (ed.) *The Routledge Reader in Early Childhood Education*. London: Routledge.

Hope, G., Austin, R., Dismore, H., Hammond, S. and Whyte, T. (2007) 'Wild woods or urban jungle: playing it safe or freedom to roam', *Education 3–13*, 35(4): 321–32.

House of Commons (2010) *Transforming Education Outside the Classroom: Sixth Report of Session 2009–10 of the Children, Schools and Families Committee*. London: HMSO.

Hughes, A. (2010) *Developing Play for the Under Threes: The Treasure Basket and Heuristic Play*. Abingdon: Routledge.

Jensen, B.J. and Bullard, J.A. (2002) *Community Playthings: The Mud Center – Recapturing Childhood*. Available at: www.communityplaythings.com (accessed 17 March 2010).

Knight, S. (2009) *Forest Schools and Outdoor Play in the Early Years*. London: Sage.

Labyrinth Builders (2010) *A Brief History of the Labyrinth*. Available at: www.laby-rinthbuilders.co.uk/index.html (accessed 13 May 2010).

Lancaster, Y.P. (2010) 'Listening to young children: enabling children to be seen and heard', in G. Pugh and B. Duffy (eds) *Contemporary Issues in the Early Years*. London: Sage.

Learning and Teaching Scotland (LTS) (2010) *Curriculum for Excellence through Outdoor Learning*. Glasgow: Learning and Teaching Scotland.

Little, H. and Wyver, S. (2008) 'Outdoor play: does avoiding the risks reduce the benefits?', *Australian Journal of Early Childhood*, 33(2): 33–40.

Louv, R. (2010) *Last Child in the Woods*, 2nd edn. London: Atlantic Books.

Lucas, B. and Claxton, G. (2010) *New Kinds of Smart*, Maidenhead: Open University Press.

Mabey, R. (2007) *Food for Free*, 3rd edn. London: Collins.

Mabey, R. (2009) *Wild Cooking*. London: Vintage.

Maynard, T. (2007) 'Encounters with Forest School and Foucault: a risky business?', *Education 3–13*, 35 (4): 379–91.

Morsanyi, K., Primi, C., Francesca, C. and Handley, S. (2009) 'The effects and side-effects of statistics education: psychology students' (mis-)conceptions of probability', *Contemporary Educational Psychology*, 34(3): 210–20.

Mortlock, C. (2009) *The Spirit of Adventure*. Kendal: Outdoor Integrity Publishing.

O'Brien, L. and Murray, R. (2007) 'Forest School and its impacts on young children: case studies in Britain', *Urban Forestry and Urban Greening*, 6: 249–65. Available at: www.sciencedirect.com

Ouvry, M. (2003) *Exercising Muscles and Minds*. London: National Children's Bureau.

Pretty, J., Angus, C., Bain, M., Barton, J., Gladwell, V., Hine, R., Pilgrim, S., Sandercock, G. and Sellens, M. (2009) *Nature, Childhood, Health and Life Pathways*. Colchester: University of Essex, Available at: www.essex.ac.uk/ces/ occasionalpapers/Nature%20Childhood%20and%20Health%20iCES%20 Occ%20Paper%202009-2%20FINAL.pdf (accessed 19 May 2010).

Roberts, P. (2006) *Nurturing Creativity in Young People: A report to Government to Inform Future Policy*. London: Department for Culture, Media and Sport.

Robins, A. and Callan, S. (2009) *Managing Early Years Settings*. London: Sage.

Robinson, K. (2001) *Out of Our Minds: Learning to be Creative*. Chichester: Capstone.

Rogers, S., Pelletier, C. and Clark, A. (2009) *Research Briefing DCSF-RBX-09-06: Play and Outcomes for Children and Young People: Literature Review to Inform the National Evaluation of Play Pathfinders and Play Builders*. London: DCSF.

Ryder Richardson, G. (2006) *Creating a Space to Grow: Developing Your Outdoor Learning Environment*. London: David Fulton.

Stacey, M. (2009) *Teamwork and Collaboration in Early Years Settings*. Exeter: Learning Matters.

Steedman, C. (1983) *The Tidy House: Little Girls Writing*. London: Virago.

Tovey, H. (2007) *Playing Outdoors: Spaces and Places, Risk and Challenge*. Maidenhead: Open University Press.

Tucker, P. and Irwin, J. (2009) 'Physical activity behaviors during the preschool years', *Child Health and Education*, 1(3): 134–45.

UNICEF (1989) *UN Convention on the Rights of the Child*. Available at: www2. ohchr.org/english/law/crc.htm (accessed 16 May 2010).

Waller, T. (2007) '"The Trampoline Tree and the Swamp Monster with 18 heads": outdoor play in the Foundation Stage and Foundation Phase', *Education 3–13*, 35(4): 393–407.

Ward, J. (2008) *I Love Dirt*. Boston, MA: Shambhala Publications, Inc.

Warden, C. (2004) *The Potential of a Puddle*. Auchterader: Mindstretchers.

White, J. (2008) *Playing and Learning Outdoors*. London: Routledge.

Wimmer, M. (2007) *Creativity and Innovation – Development of Key Competences from the Perspective of Schools and Employers, Report from the Lisbon Educult Conference*.

Wilson, A. (2009) *Creativity in Primary Education*, 2nd Edn. Exeter: Learning Matters.

Wilson, R. (2008) *Nature and Young Children*. Abingdon: David Fulton.

Worthington, R. (2008) *Nature Play: Simple and Fun Ideas for All*. Bristol: Forestry Commission England.

Index